THE WORLD ALMANAC

ALMANAC

AND BOOK OF FACTS

FOR BOOKLOVERS

THE WORLD ALMANAC® AND BOOK OF FACTS FOR BOOKLOVERS

Editor: Edward A. Thomas

Editorial Director: William A. McGeveran Jr.
Director of Desktop Publishing: Elizabeth J. Lazzara
Managing Editor: Zoë Kashner
Editorial Staff: Erik C. Gopel, Vincent G. Spadafora,
Sarah Janssen, Elizabeth Sheedy
Desktop Publishing Associate: Michael Meyerhofer
Contributors: Ben Miller, Walter Kronenberg
Cover Design: Bill SMITH STUDIO

WORLD ALMANAC BOOKS®

Publisher: Ken Park
Director, Sales and Marketing: Chuck Errig
Marketing Coordinator: Julia Suarez

THE WORLD ALMANAC AND BOOK OF FACTS FOR BOOKLOVERS

Copyright © 2005 by World Almana c Education Group, Inc.
The World Almanac and The World Almanac and Book of Facts
are registered trademarks of World Almanac Education Group
Printed in the United States of America
ISBN: 0-88687-979-5

WORLD ALMANAC BOOKS®

A Division of World Almanac Education Group, Inc.
A WRC Media Company
512 Seventh Avenue
New York, NY 10018

TABLE OF CONTENTS

WRITERS

Prominent Living Writers, Their Origins & Works

Chinua Achebe (Ogidi, Nigeria), 11/16/30, novelist, poet, short-story writer. *Things Fall Apart.*

Richard Adams (Newbury, Eng.), 5/9/20, novelist. *Watership Down, The Plague Dogs.*

Edward Albee (Washington, DC), 3/12/28, playwright. *Who's Afraid of Virginia Woolf?, A Delicate Balance.*

Isabel Allende (Lima, Peru), 8/2/42, novelist. *The House of the Spirits, Daughter of Fortune.*

Dorothy Allison (Greenville, SC), 4/11/49, novelist. *Bastard Out of Carolina, Cavedweller.*

Martin Amis (Oxford, Eng.), 8/25/49, novelist, essayist. *The Rachel Papers, Yellow Dog.*

Maya Angelou (St. Louis, MO), 4/4/28, poet, memoirist. *I Know Why the Caged Bird Sings.*

Piers Anthony (Oxford, Eng.), 8/6/34, novelist. *Magic of Xanth* Series.

Jeffrey Archer (Somerset, Eng.), 4/15/40, novelist, short-story writer. *Kane and Abel.*

Oscar Arias Sanchez (Heredia, Costa Rica), 9/13/41, writer. *Pressure Groups in Costa Rica.*

John Ashbery (Rochester, NY), 7/28/27, poet. *Self-Portrait in a Convex Mirror.*

Margaret Atwood (Ottawa, Ont.), 11/18/39, novelist, poet, short-story writer. *Handmaid's Tale, The Blind Assassin.*

David Auburn (Chicago, IL), 1969, playwright. *Proof.*

Louis Auchincloss (Lawrence, NY), 9/27/17, novelist, short-story writer. *Portrait in Brownstone.*

Jean Auel (Chicago, IL), 2/18/36, novelist. *The Clan of the Cave Bear,* "Earth's Children" Series.

Paul Auster (Newark, NJ), 2/3/47, critic, novelist, poet. "New York Trilogy": *City of Glass, Ghosts, The Locked Room.*

Alan Ayckbourn (Hampstead, Eng.), 4/12/39, playwright. *House, Garden.*

Nicholson Baker (Rochester, NY), 1/7/57, novelist, writer. *Vox, Double Fold: Libraries and the Assault on Paper.*

Russell Banks (Newton, MA), 3/28/40, novelist, short-story writer. *The Sweet Hereafter.*

John Barth (Cambridge, MD), 5/27/30, novelist, short-story writer, essayist. *Giles, Goat-Boy, Lost in the Funhouse: Fiction for Print, Tape, Live Voice.*

Ann Beattie (Washington, DC), 9/8/47, novelist, short-story writer. *Chilly Scenes of Winter.*

Peter Benchley (NYC), 5/8/40, novelist. *Jaws.*

John Berendt (Syracuse, NY), 12/5/39, writer. *Midnight in the Garden of Good and Evil: A Savannah Story.*

Thomas Berger (Cincinnati, OH), 7/20/24, novelist. *Little Big Man.*

Maeve Binchy (Dalkey, Ireland), 5/28/40, novelist. *Scarlet Feather.*

Judy Blume (Elizabeth, NJ), 2/12/38, young adult writer. *Are You There God? It's Me, Margaret.*

T(homas) Coraghessan Boyle (Peekskill, NY), 12/2/48, novelist. *World's End, Water Music.*

Ray Bradbury (Waukegan, IL), 8/22/20, novelist. *The Martian Chronicles, Fahrenheit 451.*

Barbara Taylor Bradford (Leeds, Eng.), 5/10/33, novelist. *A Woman of Substance.*

Dan Brown (Exeter, NH), 6/22/64, novelist. *The Da Vinci Code.*

Rita Mae Brown (Hanover, PA), 11/28/44, novelist, poet. *Rubyfruit Jungle.*

Christopher Buckley (NYC), 09/28/52, novelist, satirist. *The White House Mess, Thank You for Smoking.*

James Lee Burke (Houston, TX), 12/5/36, novelist. *The Lost Get-Back Boogie.*

Augusten Burroughs (Pittsburgh, PA), 1965, memoirist. *Running With Scissors: A Memoir.*

Robert Olen Butler (Granite City, IL), 1/20/45, novelist. *A Good Scent From a Strange Mountain.*

A(ntonia) S(usan Drabble) Byatt (Sheffield, England), 8/24/36, novelist, short-story writer. *Possession, Angels and Insects.*

Hortense Calisher (NYC), 12/20/11, novelist, short-story writer, memoirist. *Herself: An Autobiographical Work.*

Ethan Canin (Ann Arbor, MI), 7/19/60, novelist, short-story writer. *Emperor of the Air, The Palace Thief: Stories.*

Peter Carey (BacchusMarsh, Victoria, Australia), 5/7/43, novelist, short-story writer. *Oscar and Lucinda, True History of the Kelly Gang.*

Anne Carson (Toronto, ON) 6/21/50, poet, *Men in the Off Hours*

Caleb Carr (NYC), 08/02/55, novelist. *The Alienist.*

Michael Chabon (Washington, DC), 5/19/63, novelist. *The Amazing Adventures of Kavalier & Clay.*

Tracy Chevalier (Washington, DC), 10/62, novelist. *Girl With a Pearl Earring.*

Sandra Cisneros (Chicago, IL), 12/20/54, novelist, poet. *The House on Mango Street.*

Tom Clancy (Baltimore, MD), 4/12/47, novelist. *The Hunt for Red October, Patriot Games.*

Mary Higgins Clark (NYC), 12/24/29, novelist. *A Stranger is Watching.*

Arthur C. Clarke (Minehead, Eng.), 12/16/17, novelist, short-story writer. *2001: A Space Odyssey.*

Beverly Cleary (McMinnville, OR), 4/12/16, children's writer. *Ramona Quimby series.*

Paulo Coelho (Rio de Janeiro, Brazil), 8/24/47, novelist. *The Alchemist.*

J(ohn) M(axwell) Coetzee (Capetown, S. Africa), 2/9/40, novelist, essayist, short-story writer. *Disgrace.*

Billy Collins (NYC), 3/22/41, poet *Sailing Alone Around the Room.*

Jackie Collins (London, Eng.), 10/4/41, novelist. *Hollywood Wives.*

Evan S. Connell (Kansas City, MO), 8/17/24, writer. *Son of the Morning Star: Custer and the Little Bighorn.*

Pat Conroy (Atlanta, GA), 10/26/45, novelist. *The Prince of Tides.*

Robin Cook (NYC), 5/4/40, novelist. *Coma.*

Patricia Cornwell (Miami, FL), 6/9/56, novelist. *Postmortem.*

Harry Crews (Alma, GA), 6/6/35, novelist. *The Gospel Singer.*

Michael Crichton (Chicago, IL), 10/23/42, novelist. *The Andromeda Strain, Jurassic Park.*

Michael Cunningham (Cincinnati, Ohio), 11/6/52, novelist. *The Hours.*

Don DeLillo (NYC), 11/20/36, novelist. *White Noise, Underworld.*

Nelson DeMille (NYC), 8/23/43, novelist. *The General's Daughter.*

Joan Didion (Sacramento, CA), 12/5/34, novelist, essayist. *Slouching Toward Bethlehem.*

E(dgar) L(aurence) Doctorow (NYC), 1/6/31, novelist. *The Book of Daniel, Ragtime.*

Takako Doi (Hyogo, Jap.), 11/30/28, writer. *Doi Takako My Way.*

Rita Dove (Akron, OH), 8/28/52, poet. *On the Bus with Rosa Parks: Poems.*

Roddy Doyle (Dublin, Ireland), 5/8/58, novelist. *Paddy Clark Ha Ha Ha.*

Umberto Eco (Alessandria, Italy), 1/5/32, novelist. *Foucault's Pendulum, The Name of the Rose.*

Bret Easton Ellis (Los Angeles, CA), 3/7/64, novelist. *Less Than Zero, American Psycho.*

James Ellroy (Los Angeles), 3/4/48, novelist. *L.A. Confidential.*

Louise Erdrich (Little Falls, MN), 6/7/54, novelist. *Love Medicine, The Beet Queen.*

Laura Esquivel (Mexico City, Mexico), 9/30/51, novelist. *Like Water for Chocolate.*

Jeffrey Eugenides (Grosse Point, MI), 1960, novelist. *The Virgin Suicides, Middlesex.*

Lawrence Ferlinghetti (Yonkers, NY), 3/24/19, poet, novelist. *A Coney Island of the Mind.*

Helen Fielding (Morley, Yorkshire, Eng.), 02/19/58, novelist. *Bridget Jones's Diary.*

Ken Follett (Cardiff, Wales), 6/5/49, novelist. *Eye of the Needle.*

Dario Fo (San Giano, Italy), 3/26/26, playwright. *Accidental Death of an Anarchist.*

Horton Foote (Wharton, TX), 3/14/16, playwright. *The Trip to Bountiful.*

Richard Ford (Jackson, MS), 2/16/44, novelist. *Independence Day.*

Frederick Forsyth (Ashford, Eng.), 8/25/38, novelist. *The Day of the Jackal.*

John Fowles (Leigh-on-Sea, Eng.), 3/31/26, novelist. *The French Lieutenant's Woman.*

Paula Fox (NYC), 4/22/23, children's writer. *A Place Apart, One-Eyed Cat.*

Dick Francis (Tenby, Pembrokeshire, Wales), 10/31/20, novelist. *Come to Grief.*

Jonathan Franzen (Western Springs, IL), 8/17/59, novelist. *The Corrections.*

Michael Frayn (London, Eng.), 9/8/33, novelist, playwright. *Copenhagen, Democracy.*

Charles Frazier (Asheville, NC), 11/04/50, novelist. *Cold Mountain.*

Marilyn French (NYC), 11/21/29, novelist. *The Women's Room.*

Brian Friel (Omagh, County Tyrone, N. Ireland), 1/9/29, playwright. *Dancing at Lughnasa.*

Carlos Fuentes (Panama City, Panama), 11/11/28, novelist. *Where the Air Is Clear.*

Ernest J. Gaines (Oscar, LA), 1/15/33, novelist. *The Autobiography of Miss Jane Pittman.*

Gabriel García Márquez (Aracataca, Colombia), 3/6/28, novelist, short-story writer. *One Hundred Years of Solitude.*

Frank Gilroy (Bronx, NY), 10/13/25, playwright. *The Subject Was Roses.*

Gail Godwin (Birmingham, AL), 6/18/37, novelist. *The Odd Woman, A Mother and Two Daughters.*

William Goldman Chicago, IL), 8/12/31, novelist. *Marathon Man, The Princess Bride.*

Nadine Gordimer (Springs, S. Africa), 11/20/23, novelist. *The Conservationist.*

Mary Gordon (Far Rockaway, Long Island, NY), 12/8/49, novelist. *The Company of Women.*

Sue Grafton (Louisville, KY), 4/24/40, novelist. The Kinsey Millhone Alphabet Mystery series.

Günter Grass (Danzig, now Gdansk, Poland), 10/16/27, novelist, playwright, poet. *The Tin Drum.*

Shirley Ann Grau (New Orleans, LA), 7/8/29, novelist. *The Keepers of the House.*

John Grisham (Jonesboro, AR), 2/8/55, novelist. *A Time To Kill, The Firm.*

John Guare (NYC), 2/5/38, playwright. *Six Degrees of Separation.*

Daniel Handler (*Lemony Snicket*) (San Francisco, CA), 09/14/52, children's writer. *A Series of Unfortunate Events* series.

David Hare (St. Leonards, Sussex, Eng.), 6/5/47, playwright. *Plenty.*

Thomas Harris (Jackson, MS), c. 1947, novelist. *Silence of the Lambs.*

Jim Harrison (Grayling, MI), 12/11/37, novelist, poet. *Legends of the Fall.*

Robert Hass (San Francisco, CA), 3/1/41, poet. *Twentieth Century Pleasures: Prose on Poetry.*

Vaclav Havel (Prague, Czech.), 10/5/36, playwright, poet. *The Garden Party, The Memorandum.*

Seamus Heaney (Mossbawn, Cty. Derry, N. Ireland), 4/13/39, poet, essayist. *Beowulf: A New Verse Translation.*

Mark Helprin (NYC), 6/28/47, novelist, short-story writer. *Winter's Tale, A Soldier of the Great War.*

Carl Hiaasen (S. Florida), 3/12/53, novelist. *Tourist Season, Strip Tease.*

Oscar Hijuelos (NYC), 8/24/51, novelist, short-story writer. *The Mambo Kings Play Songs of Love.*

Tony Hillerman (Sacred Heart, OK), 5/27/25, novelist. *Dance Hall of the Dead.*

S(usan) E(loise) Hinton (Tulsa, OK), 7/22/50 young adult writer. *The Outsiders.*

Alice Hoffman (NYC), 3/16/52, novelist. *The Drowning Season.*

John Irving (Exeter, NH), 3/2/42, novelist. *The World According to Garp, A Prayer for Owen Meany.*

Kazuo Ishiguro (Nagasaki, Japan), 11/8/54, novelist. *The Remains of the Day.*

John Jakes (Chicago, IL), 3/31/32, novelist. The Bicentennial series, *North and South.*

P(hyllis) D(orothy) James (Oxford, Eng.), 8/3/20, novelist. Inspector Adam Dalgliesh mystery series.

Ha Jih (Liaoning, China), 02/21/56, novelist. *Waiting.*

Erica Jong (NYC), 3/26/42, novelist, poet. *Fear of Flying.*

Garrison Keillor (Anoka, MN), 8/7/42, humorist. *Lake Wobegon Days.*

Thomas Keneally (Sydney, Austral.), 10/7/35, novelist. *Schindler's List.*

William Kennedy (Albany, NY), 1/16/28, novelist. *Ironweed.*

Jamaica Kincaid (St. John's, Antigua), 5/25/49, novelist, nonfiction writer. *The Autobiography of My Mother.*

Stephen King (Portland, ME), 9/21/47, novelist, short-story writer. *Carrie, The Shining, The Stand.*

Barbara Kingsolver (Annapolis, MD), 4/8/55, novelist, short-story writer. *The Poisonwood Bible.*

Maxine Hong Kingston (Stockton, CA), 10/27/40, memoirist. *The Woman Warrior: Memoirs of a Girlhood among Ghosts.*

Galway Kinnell (Providence, RI), 2/1/27, poet. *When One Has Lived a Long time Alone.*

Dean Koontz (Everett, PA), 7/9/45, novelist. *Demon Seed.*

Ted Kooser (Ames, IA), 4/25/39, poet. (U.S. poet laureate), *Delights & Shadows.*

Judith Krantz (NYC), 1/9/28, novelist. *Scruples.*

Maxine Kumin (Philadelphia, PA), 6/6/25, poet. *Up Country: Poems of New England, New and Selected.*

Milan Kundera (Brno, Czechoslovakia), 4/1/29, novelist. *The Unbearable Lightness of Being.*

Stanley Kunitz (Worcester, MA), 7/29/05, poet. *Passing Through.*

Tony Kushner (NYC), 7/16/56, playwright. *Angels in America: Millennium Approaches.*

David Leavitt (Pittsburgh, PA), 6/23/61, novelist, short-story writer. *The Lost Language of Cranes.*

John Le Carré (Poole, Eng.), 10/19/31, novelist. *The Spy Who Came In From the Cold.*

Harper Lee (Monroeville, AL), 4/28/26, novelist. *To Kill a Mockingbird.*

Ursula K. Le Guin (Berkeley, CA), 10/21/29, novelist. *The Left Hand of Darkness.*

Madeleine L'Engle (NYC), 11/29/18, children's writer. *A Wrinkle in Time.*

Elmore Leonard (New Orleans, LA), 10/11/25, novelist. *The Hunted, Get Shorty.*

Doris Lessing (Kermanshah, Persia), 10/22/19, novelist, short-story writer. *The Golden Notebook.*

Jonathan Lethem (Brooklyn, NY), 02/19/64, novelist. *Motherless Brooklyn, Fortress of Solitude.*

Ira Levin (NYC), 8/27/29, novelist. *Rosemary's Baby, The Stepford Wives.*

David Lodge (South London, Eng.), 1/28/35, critic, novelist. *Small World, Nice Work.*

Alison Lurie (Chicago, IL), 9/3/26, novelist. *Foreign Affairs.*

Gregory Maguire (Albany, NY), 06/09/54, children's writer, novelist. *Wicked.*

Naguib Mahfouz (Cairo, Egypt), 12/11/11, novelist, playwright. *Palace Walk, Palace of Desire, Sugar Street.*

Norman Mailer (Long Branch, NJ), 1/31/23, novelist, essayist. *The Naked and the Dead, The Executioner's Song.*

David Mamet (Chicago, IL), 11/30/47, playwright. *Glengarry Glen Ross.*

Yann Martel (Salamanca, Spain), 06/25/63, novelist. *Life of Pi: A Novel.*

Bobbie Ann Mason (Mayfield, KY), 5/1/40, novelist, short-story writer. *Shiloh and Other Stories.*

Peter Matthiessen (NYC), 5/22/27, novelist, short-story, nature, travel writer. *The Snow Leopard.*

Armistead Maupin (Washington, DC), 5/13/44, novelist. *Tales of the City* Series.

Cormac McCarthy (Providence, RI), 7/20/33, novelist. *All the Pretty Horses.*

Frank McCourt (Brooklyn, NY), 8/19/30, memoirist. *Angela's Ashes.*

Colleen McCullough (Wellington, N.S.W.), 6/1/37, novelist. *The Thorn Birds.*

Alice McDermott (Brooklyn, NY), 6/27/53, novelist. *Charming Billy.*

Ian McEwan (Aldershot, England), 6/21/48, novelist. *Atonement.*

Thomas McGuane (Wyandotte, MI), 12/11/39, novelist. *Ninety-two in the Shade.*

Terry McMillan (Port Huron, MI), 10/18/51, novelist. *Waiting to Exhale.*

Larry McMurtry (Wichita Falls, TX), 6/3/36, novelist. *The Last Picture Show, Lonesome Dove.*

Terrence McNally (St. Petersburg, FL), 11/3/39, playwright. *Love! Valour! Compassion!, Master Class.*

John McPhee (Princeton, NJ), 3/8/31, writer. *Annals of the Former World.*

W(illiam) S(tanley) Merwin (NYC), 9/30/27, poet, essayist. *Travels.*

Toni Morrison (Lorain, OH), 2/18/31, novelist. *Song of Solomon, Beloved.*

Walter Mosley (Los Angeles, CA), 1/12/52, novelist. Easy Rawlins mysteries.

Andrew Motion (London, England), 10/26/52), poet (UK poet laureate). *The Price of Everything.*

Bharati Mukherjee (Calcutta, India), 7/27/40, novelist, short-story writer. *The Middleman and Other Stories.*

Alice Munro (Wingham, Ont.), 7/10/31, short-story writer. *The Love of a Good Woman.*

Haruki Murakami (Kyoto, Japan), 1/12/49, novelist. *A Wild Sheep Chase.*

V(iadiadhar) S(urajprasad) Naipaul (Chaguanas, Trinidad), 8/17/32, novelist, essayist. *A House for Mr. Biswas.*

Joyce Carol Oates (Lockport, NY), 6/16/38, novelist, short-story writer. *Black Water, Blonde.*

Edna O'Brien (Tuamgraney, Ir.), 12/15/32, novelist, short-story writer. *Lantern Slides.*

Tim O'Brien (Austin, MN), 10/1/46, novelist. *Going After Cacciato.*

Kenzaburo Oe (Uchiko, Japan), 1/31/35, novelist. *Shiiku.*

Michael Ondaatje (Colombo, Sri Lanka), 9/12/43, novelist. *The English Patient.*

Cynthia Ozick (NYC), 4/17/28, novelist, playwright, short-story writer. *The Pagan Rabbi, and Other Stories.*

Grace Paley (NYC), 12/11/22, short-story writer, poet. *The Little Disturbances of Man.*

Robert B. Parker (Springfield, MA), 9/17/32, novelist. *Promised Land,* Spenser detective series.

Suzan-Lori Parks (Fort Knox, KY), 5/10/63, playwright. *Topdog/Underdog.*

Marge Piercy (Detroit, MI), 3/31/36, novelist, poet. *The Moon Is Always Female.*

Robert Pinsky (Long Branch, NJ), 10/20/40, poet. *The Figured Wheel: New and Collected Poems 1966-1996.*

Harold Pinter (Hackney, East London, Eng.), 10/10/30, playwright, poet. *The Caretaker, The Homecoming.*

Reynolds Price (Macon, NC), 2/1/33, novelist, poet, essayist. *The Collected Stories.*

Richard Price (Bronx, NY), 10/12/49, novelist. *The Wanderers, Clockers.*

E(dna) Annie Proulx (Norwich, CT), 8/22/35, novelist, short-story writer. *The Shipping News.*

Philip Pullman (Norwich, Eng.), 10/19/46, young adult novelist, *Northern Lights.*

Thomas Pynchon (Glen Cove, Long Island, NY), 5/8/37, novelist. *V., Mason & Dixon.*

David Rabe (Dubuque, IA), 3/10/40, playwright, *Hurlyburly.*

Ishmael Reed (Chattanooga, TN), 2/22/38, novelist, poet. *Mumbo Jumbo.*

Ruth Rendell (London, England), 2/17/30, novelist. Inspector Wexford mysteries.

Anne Rice (New Orleans, LA), 10/4/41, novelist. *Interview With the Vampire.*

Adrienne Rich (Baltimore, MD), 5/16/29, poet. *Diving Into the Wreck.*

Nora Roberts (Washington, DC), 10/10/50, novelist. *Three Fates.*

Philip Roth (Newark, NJ), 3/19/33, novelist. *Portnoy's Complaint, American Pastoral.*

J(oanne) K(athleen) Rowling (Chipping Sodbury, Eng.), 7/31/65, novelist. *Harry Potter* series.

Norman Rush (Oakland, CA), 10/24/33, novelist. *Mating.*

Salman Rushdie (Bombay, India), 6/19/47, novelist, essayist. *Midnight's Children, The Satanic Verses.*

Richard Russo (Johnstown, NY), 7/15/49, novelist. *Nobody's Fool, Empire Falls.*

J(erome) D(avid) Salinger (NYC), 1/1/19, novelist, short-story writer. *The Catcher in the Rye.*

José Saramago (Azinhaga, Portugal), 11/16/22, novelist, playwright, poet. *Baltasar and Blimunda.*

Alice Sebold (Madison, WI), 1963, novelist. *The Lovely Bones.*

David Sedaris (Johnson City, NY), 12/26/56, essayist. *Me Talk Pretty One Day.*

Vikram Seth (Calcutta, India), 6/20/52, short-story writer. *The Golden Gate: A Novel in Verse.*

Sidney Sheldon (Chicago, IL), 2/11/17, novelist. *The Other Side of Midnight.*

Sam Shepard (Ft. Sheridan, IL), 11/5/43, playwright. *Buried Child, True West.*

Charles Simic (Belgrade, Yugoslavia), 5/9/38, poet, essayist. *Walking the Black Cat.*

Neil Simon (Bronx, NY), 7/4/27, playwright. *The Odd Couple, The Sunshine Boys, Lost in Yonkers.*

Jane Smiley (Los Angeles, CA), 9/26/49, novelist. *A Thousand Acres.*

Gary Snyder (San Franscisco, CA), 5/8/30, poet. *Turtle Island.*

Aleksandr Solzhenitsyn (Kislovodsk, Russia), 12/11/18, novelist, dramatist, historian. *The Gulag Archipelago.*

Wole Soyinka (Abeokuta, Nigeria), 7/13/34, playwright, poet. *A Play of Giants.*

Mickey Spillane (Brooklyn, NY), 3/9/18, novelist. Mike Hammer detective series.

Danielle Steel (NYC), 8/14/47, novelist. *Mixed Blessings.*

Richard Stern (NYC), 2/25/28, novelist, short-story writer. *Stitch.*

Mary Stewart (Sunderland, Eng.), 9/17/16, novelist. The Merlin Trilogy.

R(obert) L(awrence) Stine (Columbus, OH), 10/8/43, children's writer. *Goosebump* series.

Tom Stoppard (Zlin, Czech.), 7/3/37, playwright. *Rosencrantz and Guildenstern Are Dead.*

Mark Strand (Sumerside, PEI, Canada), 4/11/34, poet, *Blizzard of One.*

William Styron (Newport News, VA), 6/11/25, novelist. *The Confessions of Nat Turner, Sophie's Choice.*

Wislawa Szymborska (Kornik, Poland), 7/2/23, poet. *View With a Grain of Sand.*

Amy Tan (Oakland, CA), 2/19/52, novelist. *The Joy Luck Club.*

Donna Tartt (Greenwood, MS), 12/23/63, novelist. *The Secret History.*

Paul Theroux (Medford, MA), 4/10/41, novelist, travel writer. *The Mosquito Coast.*

Calvin Trillin (Kansas City, MO), 12/5/35, essayist, humorist. *Travels With Alice.*

Scott F. Turow (Chicago, IL), 4/12/49, novelist. *Presumed Innocent.*

Anne Tyler (Minneapolis, MN), 10/25/41, novelist. *The Accidental Tourist.*

John Updike (Shillington, PA), 3/18/32, novelist, short-story writer, poet, essayist. *Rabbit Is Rich, Rabbit at Rest, The Witches of Eastwick.*

Mario Vargas Llosa (Arequipa, Peru), 3/28/36, novelist. *The Time of the Hero.*

Gore Vidal (West Point, NY), 10/3/25, essayist, novelist. *Myra Breckinridge, Lincoln.*

Paula Vogel (Washington, DC), 11/16/51, playwright. *How I Learned to Drive.*

Kurt Vonnegut Jr. (Indianapolis, IN), 11/11/22, novelist, short-story writer. *Slaughterhouse-Five, Breakfast of Champions.*

Derek Walcott (Castries, Saint Lucia), 1/23/30, poet. *Omeros, 1948-1984.*

Alice Walker (Eatonton, GA), 2/9/44, novelist, poet. *The Color Purple.*

Robert James Waller (Rockford, IA), 8/1/39, novelist; essayist. *The Bridges of Madison County.*

Joseph Wambaugh (East Pittsburgh, PA), 1/22/37, novelist, nonfiction writer. *The Onion Field.*

Wendy Wasserstein (Brooklyn, NY), 10/18/50, playwright. *The Heidi Chronicles.*

Edmund White (Cincinnati, OH), 1/19/40, novelist. *A Boy's Own Story, The Beautiful Room Is Empty.*

C(harles) K(enneth) Williams (Newark, NJ), 11/4/36, poet. *The Singing.*

August Wilson (Pittsburgh, PA), 4/27/45, playwright. *Fences, The Piano Lesson.*

Lanford Wilson (Lebanon, MO), 4/13/37, playwright. *Talley's Folly.*

Tom Wolfe (Richmond, VA), 3/2/31, novelist, essayist. *The Right Stuff, The Bonfire of the Vanities.*

Tobias Wolff (Birmingham, AL), 6/19/45, memoirist, novelist, short-story writer. *This Boy's Life: A Memoir.*

Herman Wouk (NYC), 5/27/15, novelist. *The Caine Mutiny.*

Yevgeny Yevtushenko (Irkutsk, Russia), 7/18/33, novelist, poet. *Wild Berries.*

Notable Writers of the Past, Their Origins & Works

Alice Adams, 1926-99, (U.S.) novelist, short-story writer. *Superior Woman.*

James Agee, 1909-55, (U.S.) novelist. *A Death in the Family.*

S(hmuel) Y(osef) Agnon, 1888-1970, (Is.) Hebrew novelist. *Only Yesterday.*

Conrad Aiken, 1889-1973, (U.S.) poet, critic. *Ushant.*

Anna Akhmatova, 1889-1966, (Russ.) poet. *Requiem.*

Louisa May Alcott, 1832-88, (U.S.) novelist. *Little Women.*

Sholom Aleichem, 1859-1916, (Russ.) Yiddish writer. *Tevye's Daughters, The Old Country.*

Vicente Aleixandre, 1898-1984, (Sp.) poet. *La destrucción o el amor, Dialogolos del conocimiento.*

Horatio Alger, 1832-1899, (U.S.) "rags-to-riches" books.

Jorge Amado, 1912-2001, (Brazil) novelist. *Dona Flor and Her Two Husbands, The Violent Land.*

Eric Ambler, 1909-98, (Br.) suspense novelist. *A Coffin for Dimitrios.*

Kingsley Amis, 1922-95, (Br.) novelist, critic. *Lucky Jim.*

Hans Christian Andersen, 1805-75, (Dan.) author of fairy tales. *The Ugly Duckling.*

Maxwell Anderson, 1888-1959, (U.S.) playwright. *What Price Glory?, High Tor, Winterset, Key Largo.*

Sherwood Anderson, 1876-1941, (U.S.) short-story writer. "Death in the Woods"; *Winesburg, Ohio.*

Reinaldo Arenas, 1943-1990, (Cuba) short-story writer, novelist. *Before Night Falls.*

Ludovico Ariosto, 1474-1533, (It.) poet. *Orlando Furioso.*

Matthew Arnold, 1822-88, (Br.) poet, critic. "Thrysis," "Dover Beach," "Culture and Anarchy."

Isaac Asimov, 1920-92, (U.S.) versatile writer, espec. of science fiction. *I Robot.*

Miguel Angel Asturias, 1899-1974, (Guatemala) novelist. *El Señor Presidente.*

W(ystan) H(ugh) Auden, 1907-73, (Br.) poet, playwright, literary critic. "The Age of Anxiety."

Jane Austen, 1775-1817, (Br.) novelist. *Pride and Prejudice, Sense and Sensibility, Emma, Mansfield Park.*

Isaac Babel, 1894-1941, (Russ.) short-story writer, playwright. *Odessa Tales, Red Cavalry.*

James Baldwin, 1924-87, author, playwright. *The Fire Next Time, Blues for Mister Charlie.*

Honoré de Balzac, 1799-1850, (Fr.) novelist. *Père Goriot, Cousine Bette, Eugénie Grandet.*

James M. Barrie, 1860-1937, (Br.) playwright, novelist. *Peter Pan, Dear Brutus, What Every Woman Knows.*

Charles Baudelaire, 1821-67, (Fr.) poet. *Les Fleurs du Mal.*

L(yman) Frank Baum, 1856-1919, (U.S.) children's writer. *Wizard of Oz* series.

Simone de Beauvoir, 1908-86, (Fr.) novelist, essayist. *The Second Sex, Memoirs of a Dutiful Daughter.*

Samuel Beckett, 1906-89, (Ir.) novelist, playwright. *Waiting for Godot, Endgame* (plays); *Murphy, Watt, Molloy* (novels).

Brendan Behan, 1923-64, (Ir.) playwright. *The Quare Fellow, The Hostage, Borstal Boy.*

Saul Bellow, 1915-2005, (U.S.) novelist. *The Adventures of Augie March, Humboldt's Gift.*

Robert Benchley, 1889-1945, (U.S.) humorist.

Stephen Vincent Benét, 1898-1943, (U.S.) poet, novelist. *John Brown's Body.*

John Berryman, 1914-72, (U.S.) poet. *Homage to Mistress Bradstreet.*

Ambrose Bierce, 1842-1914, (U.S.) short-story writer, journalist. *In the Midst of Life, The Devil's Dictionary.*

Elizabeth Bishop, 1911-79, (U.S.) poet. *North and South—A Cold Spring.*

William Blake, 1757-1827, (Br.) poet, artist. *Songs of Innocence, Songs of Experience.*

Aleksandr Blok, 1880-1921, (Russ.) poet. "The Twelve," "The Scythians."

Giovanni Boccaccio, 1313-75, (It.) poet. *Decameron.*

Heinrich Böll, 1917-85, (Ger.) novelist, short-story writer. *Group Portrait With Lady.*

Jorge Luis Borges, 1900-86, (Arg.) short-story writer, poet, essayist. *Labyrinths.*

James Boswell, 1740-95, (Sc.) biographer. *The Life of Samuel Johnson.*

Pierre Boulle, (1913-94), (Fr.) novelist. *The Bridge Over the River Kwai, Planet of the Apes.*

Paul Bowles, 1910-99, (U.S.) novelist, short-story writer. *The Sheltering Sky*

Anne Bradstreet, c1612-72, (U.S.) poet. *The Tenth Muse Lately Sprung Up in America.*

Bertolt Brecht, 1898-1956, (Ger.) dramatist, poet. *The Threepenny Opera, Mother Courage and Her Children.*

Charlotte Brontë, 1816-55, (Br.) novelist. *Jane Eyre.*

Emily Brontë, 1818-48, (Br.) novelist. *Wuthering Heights.*

Elizabeth Barrett Browning, 1806-61, (Br.) poet. *Sonnets From the Portuguese, Aurora Leigh.*

Joseph Brodsky, 1940-96, (Russ.-U.S.) poet. *A Part of Speech, Less Than One, To Urania.*

Robert Browning, 1812-89, (Br.) poet. "My Last Duchess," "Fra Lippo Lippi," *The Ring and The Book.*

Pearl S. Buck, 1892-1973, (U.S.) novelist. *The Good Earth.*

Mikhail Bulgakov, 1891-1940, (Russ.) novelist, playwright. *The Heart of a Dog, The Master and Margarita.*

John Bunyan, 1628-88, (Br.) writer. *Pilgrim's Progress.*

Anthony Burgess, 1917-93, (Br.) novelist. *A Clockwork Orange.*

Frances Hodgson Burnett, 1849-1924, (Br.-U.S.) novelist. *The Secret Garden.*

Robert Burns, 1759-96, (Sc.) poet. "Flow Gently, Sweet Afton," "My Heart's in the Highlands," "Auld Lang Syne."

Edgar Rice Burroughs, 1875-1950, (U.S.) novelist. *Tarzan* books.

William S. Burroughs, 1914-97, (U.S.) novelist. *Naked Lunch.*

George Gordon, Lord Byron, 1788-1824, (Br.) poet. *Don Juan, Childe Harold's Pilgrimage, Manfred, Cain.*

Pedro Calderón de la Barca, 1600-81, (Sp.) playwright. *Life Is a Dream.*

Italo Calvino, 1923-85, (It.) novelist, short-story writer. *If on a Winter's Night a Traveler.*

Luis Vaz de Camoes, 1524?-80 (Port.) poet. *The Lusiads.*

Albert Camus, 1913-60, (Fr.) writer. *The Stranger, The Fall.*

Elias Canetti, 1905-94, (Bulg.) novelist, essayist. *Auto-Da-Fe.*

Karel Capek, 1890-1938, (Czech.) playwright, novelist, essayist. *R.U.R. (Rossum's Universal Robots).*

Truman Capote, 1924-84, (U.S.) author. *Other Voices, Other Rooms, Breakfast at Tiffany's, In Cold Blood.*

Lewis Carroll (Charles Dodgson), 1832-98, (Br.) writer, mathematician. *Alice's Adventures in Wonderland.*

Giacomo Casanova, 1725-98, (It.) adventurer, memoirist.

Willa Cather, 1873-1947, (U.S.) novelist. *O Pioneers!, My Ántonia, Death Comes for the Archbishop.*

Constantine Cavafy, 1863-1933, (Gr.) poet. "Ithaka", "Sensual Pleasures."

Camilo José Cela, 1916-2001, (Sp.) novelist. *The Family of Pascual Duarte, The Hive.*

Miguel de Cervantes Saavedra, 1547-1616, (Sp.) novelist, dramatist, poet. *Don Quixote.*

Raymond Chandler, 1888-1959, (U.S.) writer of detective fiction. Philip Marlowe series.

Geoffrey Chaucer, c1340-1400, (Br.) poet. *The Canterbury Tales, Troilus and Criseyde.*

John Cheever, 1912-82, (U.S.) novelist, short-story writer. *The Wapshot Scandal,* "The Country Husband."

Anton Chekhov, 1860-1904, (Russ.) short-story writer, dramatist. *Uncle Vanya, The Cherry Orchard, The Three Sisters.*

G(ilbert) K(eith) Chesterton, 1874-1936, (Br.) critic, novelist, relig. apologist. Father Brown series of mysteries.

Kate Chopin, 1851-1904, (U.S.) writer. *The Awakening.*

Agatha Christie, 1890-1976, (Br.) mystery writer; created Miss Marple, Hercule Poirot; *And Then There Were None, Murder on the Orient Express, Murder of Roger Ackroyd.*

James Clavell, 1924-94, (Br.-U.S.) novelist. *Shogun, King Rat.*

Jean Cocteau, 1889-1963, (Fr.) writer, visual artist, filmmaker. *The Beauty and the Beast, Les Enfants Terribles.*

Samuel Taylor Coleridge, 1772-1834, (Br.) poet, critic. "Kubla Khan," "The Rime of the Ancient Mariner."

(Sidonie) Colette, 1873-1954, (Fr.) novelist. *Claudine, Gigi.*

Wilkie Collins, 1824-89, (Br.) novelist. *The Moonstone.*

Joseph Conrad, 1857-1924, (Br.) novelist. *Lord Jim, Heart of Darkness, The Secret Agent.*

James Fenimore Cooper, 1789-1851, (U.S.) novelist. *Leatherstocking Tales, The Last of the Mohicans.*

Pierre Corneille, 1606-84, (Fr.) dramatist. *Medeé, Le Cid.*

Hart Crane, 1899-1932, (U.S.) poet. "The Bridge."

Stephen Crane, 1871-1900, (U.S.) novelist, short-story writer. *The Red Badge of Courage,* "The Open Boat."

E. E. Cummings, 1894-1962, (U.S.) poet. *Tulips and Chimneys.*

Roald Dahl, 1916-90, (Br.-U.S.) children's writer. *Charlie and the Chocolate Factory, James and the Giant Peach.*

Gabriele D'Annunzio, 1863-1938, (It.) poet, novelist, dramatist. *The Child of Pleasure, The Intruder, The Victim.*

Dante Alighieri, 1265-1321, (It.) poet. *The Divine Comedy.*

Robertson Davies, 1913-95, (Can.) novelist, playwright, essayist. Salterton, Deptford, and Cornish trilogies.

Daniel Defoe, 1660-1731, (Br.) writer. *Robinson Crusoe, Moll Flanders, Journal of the Plague Year.*

Charles Dickens, 1812-70, (Br.) novelist. *David Copperfield, Oliver Twist, Great Expectations, A Tale of Two Cities.*

Philip K. Dick, 1928-82, (U.S.) science fiction writer. *Do Androids Dream of Electric Sheep?*

James Dickey, 1923-1997, (U.S.) poet, novelist. *Deliverance.*

Emily Dickinson, 1830-86, (U.S.) lyric poet. "Because I could not stop for Death . . .," "Success is counted sweetest . . ."

Isak Dinesen (Karen Blixen), 1885-1962, (Dan.) author. *Out of Africa, Seven Gothic Tales, Winter's Tales.*

John Donne, 1573-1631, (Br.) poet, divine. *Songs and Sonnets.*

José Donoso, 1924-96, (Chil.) surreal novelist and short-story writer. *The Obscene Bird of Night.*

John Dos Passos, 1896-1970, (U.S.) novelist. *U.S.A.*

Fyodor Dostoyevsky, 1821-81, (Russ.) novelist. *Crime and Punishment, The Brothers Karamazov, The Possessed.*

Arthur Conan Doyle, 1859-1930, (Br.) novelist. Sherlock Holmes mystery stories.

Theodore Dreiser, 1871-1945, (U.S.) novelist. *An American Tragedy, Sister Carrie.*

John Dryden, 1631-1700, (Br.) poet, dramatist, critic. *All for Love, MacFlecknoe, Absalom and Achitophel.*

Alexandre Dumas, 1802-70, (Fr.) novelist, dramatist. *The Three Musketeers, The Count of Monte Cristo.*

Alexandre Dumas (fils), 1824-95, (Fr.) dramatist, novelist. *La Dame aux Camélias, Le Demi-Monde.*

Lawrence Durrell, 1912-90, (Br.) novelist, poet. *Alexandria Quartet.*

Ilya G. Ehrenburg, 1891-1967, (Russ.) writer. *The Thaw.*

George Eliot (Mary Ann or Marian Evans), 1819-80, (Br.) novelist. *Silas Marner, Middlemarch.*

T(homas) S(tearns) Eliot, 1888-1965, (Br.) poet, critic. *The Waste Land,* "The Love Song of J. Alfred Prufrock."

Stanley Elkin, 1930-95, (U.S.) novelist, short story writer. *George Mills.*

Ralph Ellison, 1914-94, (U.S.), writer. *Invisible Man.*

Ralph Waldo Emerson, 1803-82, (U.S.) poet, essayist. "Brahma," "Nature," "The Over-Soul," "Self-Reliance."

James T. Farrell, 1904-79, (U.S.) novelist. *Studs Lonigan.*

William Faulkner, 1897-1962, (U.S.) novelist. *Sanctuary, Light in August, The Sound and the Fury, Absalom, Absalom!*

Edna Ferber, 1887-1968, (U.S.) novelist, short-story writer, playwright. *So Big, Cimarron, Show Boat.*

Henry Fielding, 1707-54, (Br.) novelist. *Tom Jones.*

F(rancis) Scott Fitzgerald, 1896-1940, (U.S.) short-story writer, novelist. *The Great Gatsby, Tender Is the Night.*

Gustave Flaubert, 1821-80, (Fr.) novelist. *Madame Bovary.*

Ian Fleming, 1908-64, (Br.) novelist; James Bond spy thrillers. *Dr. No, Goldfinger.*

Ford Madox Ford, 1873-1939, (Br.) novelist, critic, poet. *The Good Soldier.*

C(ecil) S(cott) Forester, 1899-1966, (Br.) writer. Horatio Hornblower books.

E(dward) M(organ) Forster, 1879-1970, (Br.) novelist. *A Passage to India, Howards End.*

Anatole France, 1844-1924, (Fr.) writer. *Penguin Island, My Friend's Book, The Crime of Sylvestre Bonnard.*

Robert Frost, 1874-1963, (U.S.) poet. "Birches," "Fire and Ice," "Stopping by Woods on a Snowy Evening."

William Gaddis, 1922-98, (U.S.) novelist. *The Recognitions.*

John Galsworthy, 1867-1933, (Br.) novelist, dramatist. *The Forsyte Saga.*

Federico García Lorca, 1898-1936, (Sp.) poet, dramatist. *Blood Wedding.*

Erle Stanley Gardner, 1889-1970, (U.S.) mystery writer; created Perry Mason.

Jean Genet, 1911-86, (Fr.) playwright, novelist. *The Maids.*

Kahlil Gibran, 1883-1931, (Lebanese-U.S.) mystical novelist, essayist, poet. *The Prophet.*

André Gide, 1869-1951, (Fr.) writer. *The Immoralist, The Pastoral Symphony, Strait Is the Gate.*

Allen Ginsberg, 1926-1997, (U.S.) Beat poet. "Howl."

Jean Giraudoux, 1882-1944, (Fr.) novelist, dramatist. *Electra, The Madwoman of Chaillot, Ondine, Tiger at the Gate.*

Johann Wolfgang von Goethe, 1749-1832, (Ger.) poet, dramatist, novelist. *Faust, Sorrows of Young Werther.*

Nikolai Gogol, 1809-52, (Russ.) short-story writer, dramatist, novelist. *Dead Souls, The Inspector General.*

William Golding, 1911-93, (Br.) novelist. *Lord of the Flies.*

Oliver Goldsmith, 1728-74, (Br.-Ir.) dramatist, novelist. *The Vicar of Wakefield, She Stoops to Conquer.*

Maxim Gorky, 1868-1936, (Russ.) dramatist, novelist. *The Lower Depths.*

Robert Graves, 1895-1985, (Br.) poet, classical scholar, novelist. *I, Claudius; The White Goddess.*

Thomas Gray, 1716-71, (Br.) poet. "Elegy Written in a Country Churchyard," "The Progress of Poesy."

Julien Green, 1900-98, (U.S.-Fr.) expatriate American, French novelist. *Moira, Each Man in His Darkness.*

Graham Greene, 1904-91, (Br.) novelist. *The Power and the Glory, The Heart of the Matter, The Ministry of Fear.*

Zane Grey, 1872-1939, (U.S.) writer of Western stories.

Jakob Grimm, 1785-1863, (Ger.) philologist, folklorist; with brother **Wilhelm,** 1786-1859, collected *Grimm's Fairy Tales.*

Alex Haley, 1921-92, (U.S.) author. *Roots.*

Arthur Hailey, 1920-2004, (Br.) novelist. *Hotel, Airport.*

Dashiell Hammett, 1894-1961, (U.S.) detective-story writer; created Sam Spade. *The Maltese Falcon, The Thin Man.*

Knut Hamsun, 1859-1952 (Nor.) novelist. *Hunger.*

Thomas Hardy, 1840-1928, (Br.) novelist, poet. *The Return of the Native, Tess of the D'Urbervilles, Jude the Obscure.*

Joel Chandler Harris, 1848-1908, (U.S.) Uncle Remus stories.

Moss Hart, 1904-61, (U.S.) playwright. *Once in a Lifetime, You Can't Take It With You, The Man Who Came to Dinner.*

Bret Harte, 1836-1902, (U.S.) short-story writer, poet. *The Luck of Roaring Camp.*

Jaroslav Hasek, 1883-1923, (Czech.) writer, playwright. *The Good Soldier Schweik.*

John Hawkes, 1925-98, (U.S.) experimental fiction writer. *The Goose on the Grave, Blood Oranges.*

Nathaniel Hawthorne, 1804-64, (U.S.) novelist, short-story writer. *The Scarlet Letter,* "Young Goodman Brown."

Heinrich Heine, 1797-1856, (Ger.) poet. *Book of Songs.*

Robert Heinlein, 1907-88, (U.S.) science fiction writer. *Stranger in a Strange Land.*

Joseph Heller, 1923-99, (U.S.) novelist. *Catch-22.*

Lillian Hellman, 1905-84, (U.S.) playwright, author of memoirs. *The Little Foxes, An Unfinished Woman, Pentimento.*

Ernest Hemingway, 1899-1961, (U.S.) novelist, short-story writer. *A Farewell to Arms, For Whom the Bell Tolls.*

O. Henry (W. S. Porter), 1862-1910, (U.S.) short-story writer. "The Gift of the Magi."

George Herbert, 1593-1633, (Br.) poet. "The Altar," "Easter Wings."

Zbigniew Herbert, 1924-98, (Pol.) poet. "Apollo and Marsyas."

Robert Herrick, 1591-1674, (Br.) poet. "To the Virgins, to Make Much of Time."

James Herriot (James Alfred Wight), 1916-95, (Br.) novelist, veterinarian. *All Creatures Great and Small.*

John Hersey, 1914-93, (U.S.) novelist, journalist. *Hiroshima, A Bell for Adano.*

Hermann Hesse, 1877-1962, (Ger.) novelist, poet. *Death and the Lover, Steppenwolf, Siddhartha.*

James Hilton, 1900-54, (Br.) novelist. *Lost Horizon.*

Oliver Wendell Holmes, 1809-94, (U.S.) poet, novelist. *The Autocrat of the Breakfast-Table.*

Gerard Manley Hopkins, 1844-89, (Br.) poet. "Pied Beauty," "God's Grandeur."

A(lfred) E. Housman, 1859-1936, (Br.) poet. *A Shropshire Lad.*

William Dean Howells, 1837-1920, (U.S.) novelist, critic. *The Rise of Silas Lapham.*

Langston Hughes, 1902-67, (U.S.) poet, playwright. *The Weary Blues, One-Way Ticket, Shakespeare in Harlem.*

Ted Hughes, 1930-98, (Br.) British poet laureate, 1984-98. *Crow, The Hawk in the Rain.*

Victor Hugo, 1802-85, (Fr.) poet, dramatist, novelist. *Notre Dame de Paris, Les Misérables.*

Zora Neale Hurston, 1903-60, (U.S.) novelist, folklorist. *Their Eyes Were Watching God, Mules and Men.*

Aldous Huxley, 1894-1963, (Br.) writer. *Brave New World.*

Henrik Ibsen, 1828-1906, (Nor.) dramatist, poet. *A Doll's House, Ghosts, The Wild Duck, Hedda Gabler.*

William Inge, 1913-73, (U.S.) playwright. *Picnic; Come Back, Little Sheba; Bus Stop.*

Eugene Ionesco, 1910-94, (Fr.) surrealist dramatist. *The Bald Soprano, The Chairs.*

Washington Irving, 1783-1859, (U.S.) writer. "Rip Van Winkle," "The Legend of Sleepy Hollow."

Christopher Isherwood, 1904-1986, (Br.) novelist, playwright. *The Berlin Stories.*

Shirley Jackson, 1919-65, (U.S.) writer. "The Lottery."

Henry James, 1843-1916, (U.S.) novelist, short-story writer, critic. *The Portrait of a Lady, The Ambassadors, Daisy Miller.*

Robinson Jeffers, 1887-1962, (U.S.) poet, dramatist. *Tamar and Other Poems, Medea.*

Samuel Johnson, 1709-84, (Br.) author, scholar, critic. *Dictionary of the English Language, Vanity of Human Wishes.*

Ben Jonson, 1572-1637, (Br.) dramatist, poet. *Volpone.*

James Joyce, 1882-1941, (Ir.) writer. *Ulysses, Dubliners, A Portrait of the Artist as a Young Man, Finnegans Wake.*

Ernst Junger, 1895-1998, (Ger.) novelist, essayist. *The Peace, On the Marble Cliff.*

Franz Kafka, 1883-1924, (Austro-Hung./Czech) novelist, short-story writer. *The Trial, The Castle,* "The Metamorphosis."

George S. Kaufman, 1889-1961, (U.S.) playwright. *The Man Who Came to Dinner, You Can't Take It With You, Stage Door.*

Yasunari Kawabata, 1899-1972, (Japan) novelist. *The Sound of the Mountains.*

Nikos Kazantzakis, 1883-1957, (Gk.) novelist. *Zorba the Greek, A Greek Passion.*

Alfred Kazin, 1915-98 (U.S.) author, critic, teacher. *On Native Grounds.*

John Keats, 1795-1821, (Br.) poet. "Ode on a Grecian Urn," "Ode to a Nightingale," "La Belle Dame Sans Merci."

Jack Kerouac, 1922-1969, (U.S.), author, Beat poet. *On the Road, The Dharma Bums,* "Mexico City Blues."

Joyce Kilmer, 1886-1918, (U.S.) poet. "Trees."

Rudyard Kipling, 1865-1936, (Br.) author, poet. "The White Man's Burden," "Gunga Din," *The Jungle Book.*

Jean de la Fontaine, 1621-95, (Fr.) poet. *Fables choisies.*

Pär Lagerkvist, 1891-1974, (Swed.) poet, dramatist, novelist. *Barabbas, The Sybil.*

Selma Lagerlöf, 1858-1940, (Swed.) novelist. *Jerusalem, The Ring of the Lowenskolds.*

Alphonse de Lamartine, 1790-1869, (Fr.) poet, novelist, statesman. *Méditations poétiques.*

Charles Lamb, 1775-1834, (Br.) essayist. *Specimens of English Dramatic Poets, Essays of Elia.*

Giuseppe di Lampedusa, 1896-1957, (It.) novelist. *The Leopard.*

William Langland, c1332-1400, (Eng.) poet. *Piers Plowman.*

Ring Lardner, 1885-1933, (U.S.) short-story writer, humorist.

Louis L'Amour, 1908-88, (U.S.) western author, screenwriter. *Hondo, The Cherokee Trail.*

D(avid) H(erbert) Lawrence, 1885-1930, (Br.) novelist. *Sons and Lovers, Women in Love, Lady Chatterley's Lover.*

Halldor Laxness, 1902-98, (Icelandic) novelist. *Iceland's Bell.*

Mikhail Lermontov, 1814-41, (Russ.) novelist, poet. "Demon," *Hero of Our Time.*

Alain-René Lesage, 1668-1747, (Fr.) novelist. *Gil Blas de Santillane.*

Gotthold Lessing, 1729-81, (Ger.) dramatist, philosopher, critic. *Miss Sara Sampson, Minna von Barnhelm.*

C(live) S(taples) Lewis, 1898-1963, (Br.) critic, novelist, religious writer. *Allegory of Love; The Lion, the Witch and the Wardrobe; Out of the Silent Planet.*

Sinclair Lewis, 1885-1951, (U.S.) novelist. *Babbitt, Main Street, Arrowsmith, Dodsworth.*

Li Po, 701-762 (China) poet. "Song Before Drinking," "She Spins Silk."

Vachel Lindsay, 1879-1931, (U.S.) poet. *General William Booth Enters Into Heaven, The Congo.*

Hugh Lofting, 1886-1947, (Br.) writer. Dr. Doolittle series.

Jack London, 1876-1916, (U.S.) novelist, journalist. *Call of the Wild, The Sea-Wolf, White Fang.*

Henry Wadsworth Longfellow, 1807-82, (U.S.) poet. *Evangeline, The Song of Hiawatha.*

Lope de Vega, 1562-1635, (Sp.) playwright. *Noche de San Juan, Maestro de Danzar.*

H(oward) P(hillips) Lovecraft, 1890-1937, (U.S.), novelist, short-story writer. "At the Mountains of Madness."

Amy Lowell, 1874-1925, (U.S.) poet, critic. "Lilacs."

James Russell Lowell, 1819-91, (U.S.) poet, editor. *Poems, The Biglow Papers.*

Robert Lowell, 1917-77, (U.S.) poet. "Lord Weary's Castle."

Joaquim Maria Machado de Assis, 1839-1908, (Brazil) novelist, poet. *The Posthumous Memoirs of Bras Cubas.*

Archibald MacLeish, 1892-1982, (U.S.) poet. *Conquistador.*

Bernard Malamud, 1914-86, (U.S.) short-story writer, novelist. "The Magic Barrel," *The Assistant, The Fixer.*

Stéphane Mallarmé, 1842-98, (Fr.) poet. *Poésies.*

Sir Thomas Malory, ?-1471, (Br.) writer. *Le Morte d'Arthur.*

Andre Malraux, 1901-76, (Fr.) novelist. *Man's Fate.*

Osip Mandelstam, 1891-1938, (Russ.) poet. *Stone, Tristia.*

Thomas Mann, 1875-1955, (Ger.) novelist, essayist. *Buddenbrooks, The Magic Mountain,* "Death in Venice."

Katherine Mansfield, 1888-1923, (Br.) short-story writer. "Bliss."

Christopher Marlowe, 1564-93, (Br.) dramatist, poet. *Tamburlaine the Great, Dr. Faustus, The Jew of Malta.*

Andrew Marvell, 1621-78, (Br.) poet. "To His Coy Mistress."

John Masefield, 1878-1967, (Br.) poet. "Sea Fever," "Cargoes," *Salt Water Ballads.*

Edgar Lee Masters, 1869-1950, (U.S.) poet, biographer. *Spoon River Anthology.*

W(illiam) Somerset Maugham, 1874-1965, (Br.) author. *Of Human Bondage, The Moon and Sixpence.*

Guy de Maupassant, 1850-93, (Fr.) novelist, short-story writer. "A Life," "Bel-Ami," "The Necklace."

François Mauriac, 1885-1970, (Fr.) novelist, dramatist. *Viper's Tangle, The Kiss to the Leper.*

Vladimir Mayakovsky, 1893-1930, (Russ.) poet, dramatist. *The Cloud in Trousers.*

Mary McCarthy, 1912-89, (U.S.) critic, novelist, memoirist. *Memories of a Catholic Girlhood.*

Carson McCullers, 1917-67, (U.S.) novelist. *The Heart Is a Lonely Hunter, Member of the Wedding.*

Herman Melville, 1819-91, (U.S.) novelist, poet. *Moby-Dick, Typee, Billy Budd, Omoo.*

George Meredith, 1828-1909, (Br.) novelist, poet. *The Ordeal of Richard Feverel, The Egoist.*

Prosper Mérimée, 1803-70, (Fr.) author. *Carmen.*

James Merrill, 1926-95, (U.S.) poet. *Divine Comedies.*

James Michener, 1907-97, (U.S.) novelist. *Tales of the South Pacific.*

Edna St. Vincent Millay, 1892-1950, (U.S.) poet. *The Harp Weaver and Other Poems.*

Henry Miller, 1891-1980, (U.S.) erotic novelist. *Tropic of Cancer.*

Arthur Miller, 1915-2005, (U.S.) playwright. *Death of a Salesman, The Crucible, All My Sons.*

A(lan) A(lexander) Milne, 1882-1956, (Br.) author. *Winnie-the-Pooh.*

Czeslaw Milosz, 1911-2004, (Pol.) essayist, poet. "Esse," "Encounter."

John Milton, 1608-74, (Br.) poet, writer. *Paradise Lost, Comus, Lycidas, Areopagitica.*

Yukio Mishima (Hiraoka Kimitake), 1925-70, (Jpn.) writer. *Confessions of a Mask.*

Gabriela Mistral, 1889-1957, (Chil.) poet. *Sonnets of Death.*

Margaret Mitchell, 1900-49, (U.S.) novelist. *Gone With the Wind.*

Jean Baptiste Molière, 1622-73, (Fr.) dramatist. *Tartuffe, Le Misanthrope, Le Bourgeois Gentilhomme.*

Ferenc Molnár, 1878-1952, (Hung.) dramatist, novelist. *Liliom, The Guardsman, The Swan.*

Michel de Montaigne, 1533-92, (Fr.) essayist. *Essais.*

Eugenio Montale, 1896-1981, (It.) poet.

Brian Moore, 1921-99, (Ir.-U.S.) novelist. *The Lonely Passion of Judith Hearne.*

Clement C. Moore, 1779-1863, (U.S.) poet, educator. "A Visit From Saint Nicholas."

Marianne Moore, 1887-1972, (U.S.) poet.

Alberto Moravia, 1907-90, (It.) novelist, short-story writer. *The Time of Indifference.*

Sir Thomas More, 1478-1535, (Br.) writer, statesman, saint. *Utopia.*

Wright Morris, 1910-98 (U.S.) novelist. *My Uncle Dudley.*

Murasaki Shikibu (Lady Murasaki), c978-1026, (Jpn.) novelist. *The Tale of Genji.*

Iris Murdoch, 1919-99 (Br.), novelist, philosopher. *The Sea, The Sea.*

Alfred de Musset, 1810-57, (Fr.) poet, dramatist. *La Confession d'un Enfant du Siècle.*

Vladimir Nabokov, 1899-1977, (Russ.-U.S.) novelist. *Lolita, Pale Fire.*

R(aispuram) K(rishnaswami) Narayan, 1906-2001, (India), novelist, *The Guide.*

Ogden Nash, 1902-71, (U.S.) poet of light verse.

Pablo Neruda, 1904-73, (Chil.) poet. *Twenty Love Poems and One Song of Despair, Toward the Splendid City.*

Patrick O'Brian, 1914-2000, (Br.) historical novelist. *Master and Commander, Blue at the Mizzen.*

Sean O'Casey, 1884-1964, (Ir.) dramatist. *Juno and the Paycock, The Plough and the Stars.*

Frank O'Connor (Michael Donovan), 1903-66, (Ir.) short-story writer. "Guests of a Nation."

Flannery O'Connor, 1925-64, (U.S.) novelist, short-story writer. *Wise Blood,* "A Good Man Is Hard to Find."

Clifford Odets, 1906-63, (U.S.) playwright. *Waiting for Lefty, Awake and Sing, Golden Boy, The Country Girl.*

John O'Hara, 1905-70, (U.S.) novelist, short-story writer. *From the Terrace, Appointment in Samarra, Pal Joey.*

Omar Khayyam, c1028-1122, (Per.) poet. *Rubaiyat.*

Eugene O'Neill, 1888-1953, (U.S.) playwright. *Emperor Jones, Anna Christie, Long Day's Journey Into Night.*

George Orwell (Eric Arthur Blair), 1903-50, (Br.) novelist, essayist. *Animal Farm, Nineteen Eighty-Four.*

John Osborne, 1929-95, (Br.) dramatist, novelist. *Look Back in Anger, The Entertainer.*

Wilfred Owen, 1893-1918 (Br.) poet. "Dulce et Decorum Est."

Dorothy Parker, 1893-1967, (U.S.) poet, short-story writer. *Enough Rope, Laments for the Living.*

Boris Pasternak, 1890-1960, (Russ.) poet, novelist. *Doctor Zhivago.*

Alan Paton, 1903-88, (S. Africa) novelist. *Cry, the Beloved Country.*

Octavio Paz, 1914-98, (Mex.) poet, essayist. *The Labyrinth of Solitude, They Shall Not Pass!, The Sun Stone.*

Samuel Pepys, 1633-1703, (Br.) public official, diarist.

S(idney) J(oseph) Perelman, 1904-79, (U.S.) humorist. *The Road to Miltown, Under the Spreading Atrophy.*

Charles Perrault, 1628-1703, (Fr.) writer. *Tales From Mother Goose (Sleeping Beauty, Cinderella).*

Petrarch (Francesco Petrarca), 1304-74, (It.) poet. *Africa, Trionfi, Canzoniere.*

Luigi Pirandello, 1867-1936, (It.) novelist, dramatist. *Six Characters in Search of an Author.*

Sylvia Plath, 1932-63, (U.S.) author, poet. *The Bell Jar.*

Edgar Allan Poe, 1809-49, (U.S.) poet, short-story writer, critic. "Annabel Lee," "The Raven," "The Purloined Letter."

Alexander Pope, 1688-1744, (Br.) poet. *The Rape of the Lock, The Dunciad, An Essay on Man.*

Katherine Anne Porter, 1890-1980, (U.S.) novelist, short-story writer. *Ship of Fools.*

Chaim Potok, 1929-2002, (U.S.) novelist. *The Chosen.*

Ezra Pound, 1885-1972, (U.S.) poet. *Cantos.*

Anthony Powell, 1905-2000, (Br.) novelist. *A Dance to the Music of Time* series.

J(ohn) B. Priestley, 1894-1984, (Br.) novelist, dramatist. *The Good Companions.*

Marcel Proust, 1871-1922, (Fr.) novelist. *Remembrance of Things Past.*

Aleksandr Pushkin, 1799-1837, (Russ.) poet, novelist. *Boris Godunov, Eugene Onegin.*

Mario Puzo, 1920-99, (U.S.) novelist. *The Godfather.*

François Rabelais, 1495-1553, (Fr.) writer. *Gargantua.*

Jean Racine, 1639-99, (Fr.) dramatist. *Andromaque, Phèdre, Bérénice, Britannicus.*

Ayn Rand, 1905-82, (Russ.-U.S.) novelist, moral theorist. *The Fountainhead, Atlas Shrugged.*

Terence Rattigan, 1911-77, (Br.) playwright. *Separate Tables, The Browning Version.*

Erich Maria Remarque, 1898-1970, (Ger.-U.S.) novelist. *All Quiet on the Western Front.*

Samuel Richardson, 1689-1761, (Br.) novelist. *Pamela; or Virtue Rewarded.*

Rainer Maria Rilke, 1875-1926, (Ger.) poet. *Life and Songs, Duino Elegies, Poems From the Book of Hours.*

Arthur Rimbaud, 1854-91, (Fr.) poet. *A Season in Hell.*

Edwin Arlington Robinson, 1869-1935, (U.S.) poet. "Richard Cory," "Miniver Cheevy," *Merlin.*

Theodore Roethke, 1908-63, (U.S.) poet. *Open House, The Waking, The Far Field.*

Romain Rolland, 1866-1944, (Fr.) novelist, biographer. *Jean-Christophe.*

Pierre de Ronsard, 1524-85, (Fr.) poet. *Sonnets pour Hélène, La Franciade.*

Christina Rossetti, 1830-94, (Br.) poet. "When I Am Dead, My Dearest."

Dante Gabriel Rossetti, 1828-82, (Br.) poet, painter. "The Blessed Damozel."

Edmond Rostand, 1868-1918, (Fr.) poet, dramatist. *Cyrano de Bergerac.*

Damon Runyon, 1880-1946, (U.S.) short-story writer, journalist. *Guys and Dolls, Blue Plate Special.*

John Ruskin, 1819-1900, (Br.) critic, social theorist. *Modern Painters, The Seven Lamps of Architecture.*

François Sagan, (Françoise quoirez) 1935-2004, (Fr.) novelist *Bonjour Tristesse.*

Antoine de Saint-Exupéry, 1900-44, (Fr.) writer. *Wind, Sand and Stars, The Little Prince.*

Saki, or H(ector) H(ugh) Munro, 1870-1916, (Br.) writer. *The Chronicles of Clovis.*

George Sand (Amandine Lucie Aurore Dupin), 1804-76, (Fr.) novelist. *Indiana, Consuelo.*

Carl Sandburg, 1878-1967, (U.S.) poet. *The People, Yes; Chicago Poems, Smoke and Steel, Harvest Poems.*

William Saroyan, 1908-81, (U.S.) playwright, novelist. *The Time of Your Life, The Human Comedy.*

Nathalie Sarraute, 1900-99, (Fr.) Nouveau Roman novelist. *Tropismes.*

May Sarton, 1914-95, (Belg.-U.S.) poet, novelist. *Encounter in April, Anger.*

Dorothy L. Sayers, 1893-1957, (Br.) mystery writer; created Lord Peter Wimsey.

Richard Scarry, 1920-94, (U.S.) author of children's books. *Richard Scarry's Best Story Book Ever.*

Friedrich von Schiller, 1759-1805, (Ger.) dramatist, poet, historian. *Don Carlos, Maria Stuart, Wilhelm Tell.*

Sir Walter Scott, 1771-1832, (Sc.) novelist, poet. *Ivanhoe.*

Jaroslav Seifert, 1902-86, (Czech.) poet.

Dr. Seuss (Theodor Seuss Geisel), 1904-91, (U.S.) children's book author and illustrator. *The Cat in the Hat.*

William Shakespeare, 1564-1616, (Br.) dramatist, poet. *Romeo and Juliet, Hamlet, King Lear, Julius Caesar,* sonnets.

Karl Shapiro, 1913-2000, (U.S.) poet. "Elegy for a Dead Soldier."

George Bernard Shaw, 1856-1950, (Ir.-Br.) playwright, critic. *St. Joan, Pygmalion, Major Barbara, Man and Superman.*

Mary Wollstonecraft Shelley, 1797-1851, (Br.) novelist, feminist. *Frankenstein, The Last Man.*

Percy Bysshe Shelley, 1792-1822, (Br.) poet. *Prometheus Unbound, Adonais,* "Ode to the West Wind," "To a Skylark."

Richard B. Sheridan, 1751-1816, (Br.) dramatist. *The Rivals, School for Scandal.*

Robert Sherwood, 1896-1955, (U.S.) playwright, biographer. *The Petrified Forest, Abe Lincoln in Illinois.*

Mikhail Sholokhov, 1906-84, (Russ.) writer. *The Silent Don.*

Georges Simenon (Georges Sims), 1903-89, (Belg.-Fr.) mystery writer; created Inspector Maigret.

Upton Sinclair, 1878-1968, (U.S.) novelist. *The Jungle.*

Isaac Bashevis Singer, 1904-91, (Pol.-U.S.) novelist, short-story writer, in Yiddish. *The Magician of Lublin.*

C(harles) P(ercy) Snow, 1905-80, (Br.) novelist, scientist. *Strangers and Brothers, Corridors of Power.*

Susan Sontag, 1933-2004, (U.S.) essayist, novelist. "Notes on Camp," *The Volcano Lover, In America.*

Stephen Spender, 1909-95, (Br.) poet, critic, novelist. *Twenty Poems,* "Elegy for Margaret."

Edmund Spenser, 1552-99, (Br.) poet. *The Faerie Queen.*

Johanna Spyri, 1827-1901, (Swiss) children's author. *Heidi.*

Christina Stead, 1903-83, (Austral.) novelist, short-story writer. *The Man Who Loved Children.*

Richard Steele, 1672-1729, (Br.) essayist, playwright, began the *Tatler* and *Spectator. The Conscious Lovers.*

Gertrude Stein, 1874-1946, (U.S.) writer. *Three Lives.*

John Steinbeck, 1902-68, (U.S.) novelist. *The Grapes of Wrath, Of Mice and Men, The Winter of Our Discontent.*

Stendhal (Marie Henri Beyle), 1783-1842, (Fr.) novelist. *The Red and the Black, The Charterhouse of Parma.*

Laurence Sterne, 1713-68, (Br.) novelist. *Tristram Shandy.*

Wallace Stevens, 1879-1955, (U.S.) poet. *Harmonium, The Man With the Blue Guitar, Notes Toward a Supreme Fiction.*

Robert Louis Stevenson, 1850-94, (Br.) novelist, poet, essayist. *Treasure Island, A Child's Garden of Verses.*

Bram Stoker, 1845-1910, (Br.) writer. *Dracula.*

Rex Stout, 1886-1975, (U.S.) mystery writer; created Nero Wolfe.

Harriet Beecher Stowe, 1811-96, (U.S.) novelist. *Uncle Tom's Cabin.*

Lytton Strachey, 1880-1932, (Br.) biographer, critic. *Eminent Victorians, Queen Victoria, Elizabeth and Essex.*

August Strindberg, 1849-1912, (Swed.) dramatist, novelist. *The Father, Miss Julie, The Creditors.*

Jonathan Swift, 1667-1745, (Br.) satirist, poet. *Gulliver's Travels,* "A Modest Proposal."

Algernon C. Swinburne, 1837-1909, (Br.) poet, dramatist. *Atalanta in Calydon.*

John M. Synge, 1871-1909, (Ir.) poet, dramatist. *Riders to the Sea, The Playboy of the Western World.*

Rabindranath Tagore, 1861-1941, (In.) author, poet. *Sadhana, The Realization of Life, Gitanjali.*

Booth Tarkington, 1869-1946, (U.S.) novelist. *Seventeen.*

Peter Taylor, 1917-94, (U.S.) novelist. A *Summons to Memphis.*

Sara Teasdale, 1884-1933, (U.S.) poet. *Helen of Troy and Other Poems, Rivers to the Sea.*

Alfred, Lord Tennyson, 1809-92, (Br.) poet. *Idylls of the King, In Memoriam,* "The Charge of the Light Brigade."

William Makepeace Thackeray, 1811-63, (Br.) novelist. *Vanity Fair, Henry Esmond, Pendennis.*

Dylan Thomas, 1914-53, (Welsh) poet. *Under Milk Wood, A Child's Christmas in Wales.*

Hunter S. Thompson, 1937-2005, (U.S.), journalist, novelist. *Fear and Loathing in Las Vegas, The Rum Diaries.*

Henry David Thoreau, 1817-62, (U.S.) writer, philosopher, naturalist. *Walden,* "Civil Disobedience."

James Thurber, 1894-1961, (U.S.) humorist; "The Secret Life of Walter Mitty," *My Life and Hard Times.*

J(ohn) R(onald) R(euel) Tolkien, 1892-1973, (Br.) writer. *The Hobbit, Lord of the Rings* trilogy.

Leo Tolstoy, 1828-1910, (Russ.) novelist, short-story writer. *War and Peace, Anna Karenina,* "The Death of Ivan Ilyich."

Lionel Trilling, 1905-75 (U.S.) critic, author, teacher. *The Liberal Imagination.*

Anthony Trollope, 1815-82, (Br.) novelist. *The Warden, Barchester Towers,* the Palliser novels.

Ivan Turgenev, 1818-83, (Russ.) novelist, short-story writer. *Fathers and Sons, First Love, A Month in the Country.*

Amos Tutuola, 1920-97, (Nigerian) novelist. *The Palm-Wine Drunkard, My Life in the Bush of Ghosts.*

Mark Twain (Samuel Clemens), 1835-1910, (U.S.) novelist, humorist. *The Adventures of Huckleberry Finn, Tom Sawyer; Life on the Mississippi.*

Sigrid Undset, 1881-1949, (Nor.) novelist, poet. *Kristin Lavransdatter.*

Paul Valéry, 1871-1945, (Fr.) poet, critic. *La Jeune Parque, The Graveyard by the Sea.*

Paul Verlaine, 1844-96, (Fr.) Symbolist poet. *Songs Without Words.*

Jules Verne, 1828-1905, (Fr.) novelist. *Twenty Thousand Leagues Under the Sea.*

François Villon, 1431-63?, (Fr.) poet. *The Lays, The Grand Testament.*

Voltaire (F.M. Arouet), 1694-1778, (Fr.) writer of "philosophical romances"; philosopher, historian; *Candide.*

Robert Penn Warren, 1905-89, (U.S.) novelist, poet, critic. *All the King's Men.*

Evelyn Waugh, 1903-66, (Br.) novelist. *The Loved One, Brideshead Revisited, A Handful of Dust.*

H(erbert) G(eorge) Wells, 1866-1946, (Br.) novelist. *The Time Machine, The Invisible Man, The War of the Worlds.*

Eudora Welty, 1909-2001, (U.S.) Southern short story writer, novelist. "Why I Live at the P.O.," "The Ponder Heart."

Rebecca West, 1893-1983, (Br.) novelist, critic, journalist. *Black Lamb and Grey Falcon.*

Edith Wharton, 1862-1937, (U.S.) novelist. *The Age of Innocence, The House of Mirth, Ethan Frome.*

E(lwyn) B(rooks) White, 1899-1985, (U.S.) essayist, novelist. *Charlotte's Web, Stuart Little.*

Patrick White, 1912-90, (Austral.) novelist. *The Tree of Man.*

T(erence) H(anbury) White, 1906-64, (Br.) author. *The Once and Future King, A Book of Beasts.*

Walt Whitman, 1819-92, (U.S.) poet. *Leaves of Grass.*

John Greenleaf Whittier, 1807-92, (U.S.) poet, journalist. *Snow-Bound.*

Oscar Wilde, 1854-1900, (Ir.) novelist, playwright. *The Picture of Dorian Gray, The Importance of Being Earnest.*

Laura Ingalls Wilder, 1867-1957, (U.S.) novelist. *Little House on the Prairie* series of children's books.

Thornton Wilder, 1897-1975, (U.S.) playwright. *Our Town, The Skin of Our Teeth, The Matchmaker.*

Tennessee Williams, 1911-83, (U.S.) playwright. *A Streetcar Named Desire, Cat on a Hot Tin Roof, The Glass Menagerie.*

William Carlos Williams, 1883-1963, (U.S.) poet, physician. *Tempers, Al Que Quiere! Paterson,* "This Is Just to Say."

Edmund Wilson, 1895-1972, (U.S.) critic, novelist. *Axel's Castle, To the Finland Station.*

P(elham) G(renville) Wodehouse, 1881-1975, (Br.-U.S.) humorist. The "Jeeves" novels, *Anything Goes.*

Thomas Wolfe, 1900-38, (U.S.) novelist. *Look Homeward, Angel; You Can't Go Home Again.*

Virginia Woolf, 1882-1941, (Br.) novelist, essayist. *Mrs. Dalloway, To the Lighthouse, A Room of One's Own.*

William Wordsworth, 1770-1850, (Br.) poet. "Tintern Abbey," "Ode: Intimations of Immortality," *The Prelude.*

Richard Wright, 1908-60, novelist, short-story writer. *Native Son, Black Boy, Uncle Tom's Children.*

Elinor Wylie, 1885-1928, (U.S.) poet. *Nets to Catch the Wind.*

William Butler Yeats, 1865-1939, (Ir.) poet, playwright. "The Second Coming," *The Wild Swans at Coole.*

Émile Zola, 1840-1902, (Fr.) novelist. *Nana, Thérèsè Raquin.*

"Literature is my Utopia. Here I am not disfranchised. No barrier of the senses shuts me out from the sweet, gracious discourse of my book-friends. They talk to me without embarrassment or awkwardness." — Helen Keller (1880-1968), U.S. author

Where Did They Live?
Author homes to visit

Alcott & Hawthorne: The Wayside - Home of Authors (Louise May
Alcott & Nathaniel Hawthorne)
455 Lexington Road
Concord, MA 01742
www.cr.nps.gov/nr/travel/pwwmh/ma47.htm

Clemens (Twain): The Mark Twain Home
351 Farmington Avenue
Hartford, CT 06105
www.marktwainhouse.org

Dickinson: The Emily Dickinson Museum
280 Main Street
Amherst, MA 01002
www.emilydickinsonmuseum.org

Hemingway: The Ernest Hemingway Home & Museum
907 Whitehead Street
Key West, FL 33040
www.hemingwayhome.com/

Ingalls Wilder: Laura Ingalls Wilder Historic Home and Museum
3068 Highway A
Mansfield, MO 65704
www.lauraingallswilderhome.com

Melville: Herman Melville's Arrowhead
780 Holmes Road
Pittsfield, MA 01201
www.mobydick.org

Poe: Edgar Allan Poe Cottage
Kingsbridge Road and the Grand Concourse
Bronx, NY 10458
www.bronxhistoricalsociety.org/index17.html

Shakespeare: Shakespeare Birthplace
Henley Street
Stratford-upon-Avon, UK CV37 6QW
www.shakespeare.org.uk

Stowe: The Harriet Beecher Stowe House and Library
77 Forest Street
Hartford, CT 06105
www.harrietbeecherstowecenter.org

Whitman: The Walt Whitman House
328 Mickle Blvd.
Camden, NJ 08103
www.nj.gov/dep/parksandforests/historic/whitman/index.html

Wolfe: Thomas Wolfe
52 North Market Street
Asheville, NC 28801
www.wolfememorial.com

Where Are They Buried?
Final resting spots of famous writers

California
Truman Capote (1924-1984), Westwood Memorial Park, Los Angeles
John Steinbeck (1902-1968), Garden of Memories, Salinas

Florida
Zora Neale Hurston (1891-1960), Garden of Heavenly Rest, Fort Pierce

Georgia
Margaret Mitchell (1900-1949), Oakland Cemetery, Atlanta

Maryland
Edgar Allan Poe (1809-1849), Westminster Presbyterian Church and Cemetery, Baltimore

Massachusetts
Harriet Beecher Stowe (1811-1896), Academy Cemetery, Andover
Henry David Thoreau (1817-1862), Sleepy Hollow Cemetery, Concord
Ralph Waldo Emerson (1803-1882), Sleepy Hollow Cemetery, Concord

Missouri
Tennessee Williams (1911-1983), Calvary Cemetery, St. Louis

New York
Clement Clarke Moore (1779-1863), Trinity Cemetery, New York
James Baldwin (1937-1987),Ferncliff Cenetery, Hartsdale
Countee Cullen (1903-1946), Woodlawn Cemetery, Bronx
Herman Melville (1819-1891), Woodlawn Cemetery, Bronx
Ayn Rand (1905-1982), Kensico Cemetery, Valhalla

Pennsylvania
Pearl S. Buck (1892-1973), Green Hills Farm, Perkasie

Denmark
Hans Christian Andersen (1805-1875), Assistens Cemetery, Copenhagen

England
Jane Austen (1775-1817), Winchester Cathedral, Winchester
Charlotte Brontë (1816-1855) & **Emily Brontë** (1818-1848), Church of Saint Michael and All Angels, Haworth, West Yorkshire
Charles Dickens (1812-1870), Westminster Abbey, London
Rudyard Kipling (1865-1936), Westminster Abbey, London
Mary Shelley (1797-1851), Saint Peter's Churchyard, Bournemouth, Dorset
Bram Stoker (1847-1912), Golders Green Crematorium, London
J.R.R. Tolkein (1892-1973), Wolvercote Cemetery, Oxford

Switzerland
Thomas Mann (1875-1955), Kiltchberg Village Cemetery, Zurich
Vladimir Nabokov (1899-1977), Cimitière de Clarens, Clarens, Vaud

Poets Laureate

There is no record of the origin of the office of Poet Laureate of England. Henry III (1216-72) reportedly had a Versificator Regis, or King's Poet, paid 100 shillings a year. Other poets said to have filled the role include Geoffrey Chaucer (d 1400), Edmund Spenser (d 1599), Ben Jonson (d 1637), and Sir William d'Avenant (d 1668).

The first official English poet laureate was John Dryden, appointed 1668, for life (as was customary). Then came Thomas Shadwell, in 1689; Nahum Tate, 1692; Nicholas Rowe, 1715; Rev. Laurence Eusden, 1718; Colley Cibber, 1730; William Whitehead, 1757; Rev. Thomas Warton, 1785; Henry James Pye, 1790; Robert Southey, 1813; William Wordsworth, 1843; Alfred, Lord Tennyson, 1850; Alfred Austin, 1896; Robert Bridges, 1913; John Masefield, 1930; C. Day Lewis, 1968; Sir John Betjeman, 1972; Ted Hughes, 1984; Andrew Motion, 1999.

In the U.S., appointment is by Librarian of Congress and is not for life: Robert Penn Warren, appointed 1986; Richard Wilbur, 1987; Howard Nemerov, 1988; Mark Strand, 1990; Joseph Brodsky, 1991; Mona Van Duyn, 1992; Rita Dove, 1993; Robert Hass, 1995; Robert Pinsky, 1997; Stanley Kunitz, 2000; Billy Collins, 2001; Louise Glück, 2003; Ted Kooser, 2004.

Pen Names

Shalom Aleichem	Solomon J. Rabinowitz
Woody Allen	Allen Stewart Konigsberg
Maya Angelou	Marguerite Johnson
Nellie Bly	Elizabeth Jane Cochrane Seaman
John le Carré	David John Moore Cornwell
Lewis Carroll	Charles Lutwidge Dodgson
Colette	Sidonie Gabrielle Colette
Amanda Cross	Carolyn Heilbrun
Isak Dinesen	Karen Blixen
Elia	Charles Lamb
George Eliot	Mary Ann or Marian Evans
Maksim Gorky	Aleksey Maksimovich Peshkov
O. Henry	William Sydney Porter
James Herriot	James Alfred Wight
P. D. James	Phyllis Dorothy James White
Ann Landers	Esther Pauline Lederer
[John] Ross Macdonald	Kenneth Millar
André Maurois	Émile Herzog
Molière	Jean Baptiste Poquelin
Toni Morrison	Chloe Anthony Wofford
Frank O'Connor	Michael Donovan
George Orwell	Eric Arthur Blair
Ellery Queen	Frederic Dannay and Manfred B. Lee
Mary Renault	Mary Challans
Anne Rice	Howard Allen O'Brien
Françoise Sagan	Françoise Quoirez
Saki	Hector Hugh Munro
George Sand	Amandine Lucie Aurore Dupin
Dr. Seuss	Theodor Seuss Geisel
Lemony Snicket	Daniel Handler
Stendhal	Marie Henri Beyle
Mark Twain	Samuel Clemens
Voltaire	François Marie Arouet

Favorite First Lines From Novels

The editors of *The World Almanac* have ranked the following as
their 10 favorite familiar first lines from novels.

1. "It was the best of times, it was the worst of times, it was the
age of wisdom, it was the age of foolishness, it was the epoch of be-
lief, it was the epoch of incredulity, it was the season of Light, it
was the season of Darkness, it was the spring of hope, it was the
winter of despair, we had everything before us, we had nothing before us, we were all going direct to Heaven, we were all going direct the other way—in short, the period was so far like the present
period, that some of its noisiest authorities insisted on its being received, for good or for evil, in the superlative degree of comparison
only." — *A Tale of Two Cities,* **Charles Dickens**

2. "Call me Ishmael." — *Moby Dick,* **Herman Melville**

3. "Happy families are all alike, but every unhappy family is unhappy in its own way." — *Anna Karenina*, **Leo Tolstoy**

4. "It is a truth universally acknowledged, that a single man in
possession of a good fortune, must be in want of a wife." — *Pride
and Prejudice,* **Jane Austen**

5. "Many years later, as he faced the firing squad, Colonel Aure-
liano Buendia was to remember that distant afternoon when his father took him to discover ice." — *One Hundred Years of Solitude,*
Gabriel García Márquez

6. "When Gregor Samsa woke up one morning from unsettling
dreams, he found himself changed into a monstrous vermin."
— *The Metamorphosis,* **Franz Kafka**

7. "Last night I dreamt I went to Manderley again." — *Rebecca,*
Daphne Du Maurier

8. "It was a bright cold day in April, and the clocks were striking
thirteen." — *1984,* **George Orwell**

9. "Whether I shall turn out to be the hero of my own life, or
whether that station will be held by anybody else, these pages must
show." — *David Copperfield,* **Charles Dickens**

10. "If you really want to hear about it, the first thing you'll
probably want to know is where I was born, and what my lousy
childhood was like, and how my parents were occupied and all before they had me, and all that David Copperfield kind of crap, but I
don't feel like going into it, if you want to know the truth." — *The
Catcher in the Rye,* **J. D. Salinger**

Quiz: Match the Book & the Character
Character

1. __Atticus Finch
2. __Big Brother
3. __Captain Ahab
4. __Celie
5. __Dorothy Gale
6. __Ebenezer Scrooge
7. __Elizabeth Bennet
8. __Fagin
9. __Hester Prynne
10. __Holden Caulfield
11. __Holly Golightly
12. __Howard Roark
13. __Ichabod Crane
14. __Ignatius J. Reilly
15. __Jean Valjean
16. __Jo March
17. __Leopold Bloom
18. __Lestat
19. __Madame Defarge
20. __Natty Bumppo
21. __Nick and Nora Charles
22. __Philip Marlowe
23. __Sam Spade
24. __Santiago
25. __Scarlett O'Hara
26. __Tom Joad

Book, Author

a. *1984*, George Orwell
b. *A Christmas Carol*, Charles Dickens
c. *A Confederacy of Dunces*, John Kennedy Toole
d. *A Tale of Two Cities*, Charles DIckens
e. *Breakfast at Tiffany's*, Truman Capote
f. *Gone With the Wind*, Margaret Mitchell
g. *Interview with the Vampire*, Anne Rice
h. *Les Miserables*, Victor Hugo
i. *Little Women*, Louisa May Alcott
j. *Moby Dick*, Herman Melville
k. *Oliver Twist,* Charles Dickens
l. *Pride and Prejudice*, Jane Austen
m. *The Big Sleep*, Raymond Chandler
n. *The Catcher in the Rye*, J.D. Salinger
o. *The Color Purple*, Alice Walker
p. *The Fountainhead*, Ayn Rand
q. *The Grapes of Wrath*, John Steinbeck
r. *The Last of the Mohicans*, James Fenimore Cooper
s. *The Legend of Sleepy Hollow*, Washington Irving
t. *The Maltese Falcon*, Dashiell Hammett
u. *The Old Man and the Sea*, Ernest Hemingway
v. *The Scarlet Letter*, Nathaniel Hawthorne
w. *The Thin Man*, Dashiell Hammett
x. *The Wizard of Oz*, L. Frank Baum
y. *To Kill A Mockingbird*, Harper Lee
z. *Ulysses*, James Joyce

BOOK AWARDS AND PRIZES

The Alfred B. Nobel Prize Winners in Literature, 1901-2004

Alfred B. Nobel (1833-96) bequeathed $9 mil, the interest on which was to be distributed yearly to those judged to have most benefited humankind in physics, chemistry, medicine-physiology, literature, and promotion of peace. Prizes were first awarded in 1901. The 1st prize in economics was awarded in 1969, funded by Sweden's central bank. Each prize is now worth about 10 mil. Swedish kroner (about $1.35 mil). If year is omitted, no award was given.

1901	Rene F. A. Sully Prudhomme, Fr.
1902	Theodor Mommsen, Ger.
1903	Bjornsterne Bjornson, Nor.
1904	Frederic Mistral, Fr.; Jose Echegaray, Span.
1905	Henryk Sienkiewicz, Pol.
1906	Giosue Carducci, It.
1907	Rudyard Kipling, Br.
1908	Rudolf C. Eucken, Ger.
1909	Selma Lagerlof, Swed.
1910	Paul J. L. Heyse, Ger.
1911	Maurice Maeterlinck, Belg.
1912	Gerhart Hauptmann, Ger.
1913	Rabindranath Tagore, India
1915	Romain Rolland, Fr.
1916	Verner von Heidenstam, Swed.
1917	Karl A. Gjellerup, Henrik Pontoppidan, Dan.
1919	Carl F. G. Spitteler, Swiss
1920	Knut Hamsun, Nor.
1921	Anatole France, Fr.
1922	Jacinto Benavente, Span.
1923	William Butler Yeats, Ir.
1924	Wladyslaw S. Reymont, Pol.
1925	George Bernard Shaw, Ir.-Br.
1926	Grazia Deledda, It.
1927	Henri Bergson, Fr.
1928	Sigrid Undset, Nor.
1929	Thomas Mann, Ger.
1930	Sinclair Lewis, U.S.
1931	Erik A. Karlfeldt, Swed.
1932	John Galsworthy, Br.
1933	Ivan A. Bunin, USSR
1934	Luigi Pirandello, It.
1936	Eugene O'Neill, U.S.
1937	Roger Martin du Gard, Fr.
1938	Pearl S. Buck, U.S.
1939	Frans E. Sillanpaa, Fin.
1944	Johannes V. Jensen, Dan.
1945	Gabriela Mistral, Chil.
1946	Hermann Hesse, Ger.-Swiss
1947	Andre Gide, Fr.
1948	T.S. Eliot, Br.
1949	William Faulkner, U.S.
1950	Bertrand Russell, Br.

1951	Pär F. Lagerkvist, Swed.
1952	Francois Mauriac, Fr.
1953	Sir Winston Churchill, Br.
1954	Ernest Hemingway, U.S.
1955	Halldor K. Laxness, Ice.
1956	Juan Ramon Jimenez, Span.
1957	Albert Camus, Fr.
1958	Boris L. Pasternak, USSR (declined)
1959	Salvatore Quasimodo, It.
1960	Saint-John Perse, Fr.
1961	Ivo Andric, Yugo.
1962	John Steinbeck, U.S.
1963	Giorgos Seferis, Gk.
1964	Jean Paul Sartre, Fr. (declined)
1965	Mikhail Sholokhov, USSR
1966	Samuel Joseph Agnon, Isr.; Nelly Sachs, Swed.
1967	Miguel Angel Asturias, Guat.
1968	Yasunari Kawabata, Jpn.
1969	Samuel Beckett, Ir.
1970	Aleksandr I. Solzhenitsyn, USSR
1971	Pablo Neruda, Chil.
1972	Heinrich Böll, Ger.
1973	Patrick White, Austral.
1974	Eyvind Johnson, Harry Edmund Martinson, Swed.
1975	Eugenio Montale, It.
1976	Saul Bellow, U.S.
1977	Vicente Aleixandre, Span.
1978	Isaac Bashevis Singer, U.S.
1979	Odysseus Elytis, Gk.
1980	Czeslaw Milosz, Pol.-U.S.
1981	Elias Canetti, Bulg.-Br.
1982	Gabriel Garcia Marquez, Colombian-Mex.
1983	William Golding, Br.
1984	Jaroslav Siefert, Czech.
1985	Claude Simon, Fr.
1986	Wole Soyinka, Nig.
1987	Joseph Brodsky, USSR-U.S.
1988	Naguib Mahfouz, Egy.
1989	Camilo José Cela, Span.
1990	Octavio Paz, Mex.
1991	Nadine Gordimer, S. Afr.
1992	Derek Walcott, W. Ind.
1993	Toni Morrison, U.S.
1994	Kenzaburo Oe, Jpn.
1995	Seamus Heaney, Ir.
1996	Wislawa Szymborska, Pol.
1997	Dario Fo, It.
1998	Jose Saramago, Por.
1999	Günter Grass, Ger.
2000	Gao Xingjian, Chin.
2001	Sir V.S. Naipaul, Br.
2002	Imre Kertész, Hung.
2003	J.M. Coetzee, S. Afr.
2004	Elfriede Jelinek, Austria

Pulitzer Prizes in Letters

Endowed by Joseph Pulitzer (1847-1911), publisher of the *New York World*, in a bequest to Columbia Univ. and awarded annually, in years shown, for work the previous year. Prizes are now $10,000 in each category. If a year is omitted, no award was given that year.

Fiction

1918 Ernest Poole, *His Family*
1919 Booth Tarkington, *The Magnificent Ambersons*
1921 Edith Wharton, *The Age of Innocence*
1922 Booth Tarkington, *Alice Adams*
1923 Willa Cather, *One of Ours*
1924 Margaret Wilson, *The Able McLaughlins*
1925 Edna Ferber, *So Big*
1926 Sinclair Lewis, *Arrowsmith* (refused prize)
1927 Louis Bromfield, *Early Autumn*
1928 Thornton Wilder, *Bridge of San Luis Rey*
1929 Julia M. Peterkin, *Scarlet Sister Mary*
1930 Oliver LaFarge, *Laughing Boy*
1931 Margaret Ayer Barnes, *Years of Grace*
1932 Pearl S. Buck, *The Good Earth*
1933 T. S. Stribling, *The Store*
1934 Caroline Miller, *Lamb in His Bosom*
1935 Josephine W. Johnson, *Now in November*
1936 Harold L. Davis, *Honey in the Horn*
1937 Margaret Mitchell, *Gone With the Wind*
1938 John P. Marquand, *The Late George Apley*
1939 Marjorie Kinnan Rawlings, *The Yearling*
1940 John Steinbeck, *The Grapes of Wrath*
1942 Ellen Glasgow, *In This Our Life*
1943 Upton Sinclair, *Dragon's Teeth*
1944 Martin Flavin, *Journey in the Dark*
1945 John Hersey, *A Bell for Adano*
1947 Robert Penn Warren, *All the King's Men*
1948 James A. Michener, *Tales of the South Pacific*
1949 James Gould Cozzens, *Guard of Honor*
1950 A. B. Guthrie Jr., *The Way West*
1951 Conrad Richter, *The Town*
1952 Herman Wouk, *The Caine Mutiny*
1953 Ernest Hemingway, *The Old Man and the Sea*
1955 William Faulkner, *A Fable*
1956 MacKinlay Kantor, *Andersonville*
1958 James Agee, *A Death in the Family*
1959 Robert Lewis Taylor, *The Travels of Jaimie McPheeters*
1960 Allen Drury, *Advise and Consent*
1961 Harper Lee, *To Kill a Mockingbird*
1962 Edwin O'Connor, *The Edge of Sadness*
1963 William Faulkner, *The Reivers*
1965 Shirley Ann Grau, *The Keepers of the House*
1966 Katherine Anne Porter, *Collected Stories*
1967 Bernard Malamud, *The Fixer*
1968 William Styron, *The Confessions of Nat Turner*

1969 N. Scott Momaday, *House Made of Dawn*
1970 Jean Stafford, *Collected Stories*
1972 Wallace Stegner, *Angle of Repose*
1973 Eudora Welty, *The Optimist's Daughter*
1975 Michael Shaara, *The Killer Angels*
1976 Saul Bellow, *Humboldt's Gift*
1978 James Alan McPherson, *Elbow Room*
1979 John Cheever, *The Stories of John Cheever*
1980 Norman Mailer, *The Executioner's Song*
1981 John Kennedy Toole, *A Confederacy of Dunces*
1982 John Updike, *Rabbit Is Rich*
1983 Alice Walker, *The Color Purple*
1984 William Kennedy, *Ironweed*
1985 Alison Lurie, *Foreign Affairs*
1986 Larry McMurtry, *Lonesome Dove*
1987 Peter Taylor, *A Summons to Memphis*
1988 Toni Morrison, *Beloved*
1989 Anne Tyler, *Breathing Lessons*
1990 Oscar Hijuelos, *The Mambo Kings Play Songs of Love*
1991 John Updike, *Rabbit at Rest*
1992 Jane Smiley, *A Thousand Acres*
1993 Robert Olen Butler, *A Good Scent From a Strange Mountain*
1994 E. Annie Proulx, *The Shipping News*
1995 Carol Shields, *The Stone Diaries*
1996 Richard Ford, *Independence Day*
1997 Steven Millhauser, *Martin Dressler: The Tale of an American Dreamer*
1998 Philip Roth, *American Pastoral*
1999 Michael Cunningham, *The Hours*
2000 Jhumpa Lahiri, *Interpreter of Maladies*
2001 Michael Chabon, *The Amazing Adventures of Kavalier & Clay*
2002 Richard Russo, *Empire Falls*
2003 Jeffrey Eugenides, *Middlesex*
2004 Edward P. Jones, *The Known World*
2005 Marilynne Robinson, *Gilead*

Drama

1918 Jesse Lynch Williams, *Why Marry?*
1920 Eugene O'Neill, *Beyond the Horizon*
1921 Zona Gale, *Miss Lulu Bett*
1922 Eugene O'Neill, *Anna Christie*
1923 Owen Davis, *Icebound*
1924 Hatcher Hughes, *Hell-Bent for Heaven*
1925 Sidney Howard, *They Knew What They Wanted*
1926 George Kelly, *Craig's Wife*
1927 Paul Green, *In Abraham's Bosom*
1928 Eugene O'Neill, *Strange Interlude*
1929 Elmer Rice, *Street Scene*
1930 Marc Connelly, *The Green Pastures*
1931 Susan Glaspell, *Alison's House*
1932 George S. Kaufman, Morrie Ryskind, and Ira Gershwin, *Of Thee I Sing*

1933 Maxwell Anderson, *Both Your Houses*
1934 Sidney Kingsley, *Men in White*
1935 Zoe Akins, *The Old Maid*
1936 Robert E. Sherwood, *Idiot's Delight*
1937 George S. Kaufman and Moss Hart, *You Can't Take It With You*
1938 Thornton Wilder, *Our Town*
1939 Robert E. Sherwood, *Abe Lincoln in Illinois*
1940 William Saroyan, *The Time of Your Life*
1941 Robert E. Sherwood, *There Shall Be No Night*
1943 Thornton Wilder, *The Skin of Our Teeth*
1945 Mary Chase, *Harvey*
1946 Russel Crouse and Howard Lindsay, *State of the Union*
1948 Tennessee Williams, *A Streetcar Named Desire*
1949 Arthur Miller, *Death of a Salesman*
1950 Richard Rodgers, Oscar Hammerstein 2nd and Joshua Logan,
South Pacific
1952 Joseph Kramm, *The Shrike*
1953 William Inge, *Picnic*
1954 John Patrick, *Teahouse of the August Moon*
1955 Tennessee Williams, *Cat on a Hot Tin Roof*
1956 Frances Goodrich and Albert Hackett, *The Diary of Anne Frank*
1957 Eugene O'Neill, *Long Day's Journey Into Night*
1958 Ketti Frings, *Look Homeward, Angel*
1959 Archibald MacLeish, *J. B.*
1960 George Abbott, Jerome Weidman, Sheldon Harnick, and Jerry
Bock, *Fiorello!*
1961 Tad Mosel, *All the Way Home*
1962 Frank Loesser and Abe Burrows, *How to Succeed in Business
Without Really Trying*
1965 Frank D. Gilroy, *The Subject Was Roses*
1967 Edward Albee, *A Delicate Balance*
1969 Howard Sackler, *The Great White Hope*
1970 Charles Gordone, *No Place to Be Somebody*
1971 Paul Zindel, *The Effect of Gamma Rays on Man-in-the-Moon
Marigolds*
1973 Jason Miller, *That Championship Season*
1975 Edward Albee, *Seascape*
1976 Michael Bennett, James Kirkwood, Nicholas Dante, Marvin
Hamlisch, and Edward Kleban, *A Chorus Line*
1977 Michael Cristofer, *The Shadow Box*
1978 Donald L. Coburn, *The Gin Game*
1979 Sam Shepard, *Buried Child*
1980 Lanford Wilson, *Talley's Folly*
1981 Beth Henley, *Crimes of the Heart*
1982 Charles Fuller, *A Soldier's Play*
1983 Marsha Norman, *'night, Mother*
1984 David Mamet, *Glengarry Glen Ross*
1985 Stephen Sondheim and James Lapine, *Sunday in the Park
With George*
1987 August Wilson, *Fences*
1988 Alfred Uhry, *Driving Miss Daisy*

1989 Wendy Wasserstein, *The Heidi Chronicles*
1990 August Wilson, *The Piano Lesson*
1991 Neil Simon, *Lost in Yonkers*
1992 Robert Schenkkan, *The Kentucky Cycle*
1993 Tony Kushner, *Angels in America: Millennium Approaches*
1994 Edward Albee, *Three Tall Women*
1995 Horton Foote, *The Young Man From Atlanta*
1996 Jonathan Larson, *Rent*
1998 Paula Vogel, *How I Learned to Drive*
1999 Margaret Edson, *Wit*
2000 Donald Margulies, *Dinner With Friends*
2001 David Auburn, *Proof*
2002 Suzan-Lori Parks, *Topdog/Underdog*
2003 Nilo Cruz, *Anna in the Tropics*
2004 Doug Wright, *I Am My Own Wife*
2005 John Patrick Shanley, *Doubt, a parable*

History (U.S.)

1917 J. J. Jusserand, *With Americans of Past and Present Days*
1918 James Ford Rhodes, *History of the Civil War*
1920 Justin H. Smith, *The War With Mexico*
1921 William Sowden Sims, *The Victory at Sea*
1922 James Truslow Adams, *The Founding of New England*
1923 Charles Warren, *The Supreme Court in United States History*
1924 Charles Howard McIlwain, *The American Revolution: A Constitutional Interpretation*
1925 Frederick L. Paxton, *A History of the American Frontier*
1926 Edward Channing, *A History of the U.S.*
1927 Samuel Flagg Bemis, *Pinckney's Treaty*
1928 V. L Parrington, *Main Currents in American Thought*
1929 Fred A. Shannon, *The Organization and Administration of the Union Army, 1861-65*
1930 Claude H. Van Tyne, *The War of Independence*
1931 Bernadotte E. Schmitt, *The Coming of the War, 1914*
1932 Gen. John J. Pershing, *My Experiences in the World War*
1933 Frederick J. Turner, *The Significance of Sections in American History*
1934 Herbert Agar, *The People's Choice*
1935 Charles McLean Andrews, *The Colonial Period of American History*
1936 Andrew C. McLaughlin, *The Constitutional History of the United States*
1937 Van Wyck Brooks, *The Flowering of New England*
1938 Paul Herman Buck, *The Road to Reunion, 1865-1900*
1939 Frank Luther Mott, *A History of American Magazines*
1940 Carl Sandburg, *Abraham Lincoln: The War Years*
1941 Marcus Lee Hansen, *The Atlantic Migration, 1607-1860*
1942 Margaret Leech, *Reveille in Washington*
1943 Esther Forbes, *Paul Revere and the World He Lived In*
1944 Merle Curti, *The Growth of American Thought*
1945 Stephen Bonsal, *Unfinished Business*
1946 Arthur M. Schlesinger Jr., *The Age of Jackson*

1947 James Phinney Baxter 3d, *Scientists Against Time*
1948 Bernard De Voto, *Across the Wide Missouri*
1949 Roy F. Nichols, *The Disruption of American Democracy*
1950 O. W. Larkin, *Art and Life in America*
1951 R. Carlyle Buley, *The Old Northwest: Pioneer Period 1815-1840*
1952 Oscar Handlin, *The Uprooted*
1953 George Dangerfield, *The Era of Good Feelings*
1954 Bruce Catton, *A Stillness at Appomattox*
1955 Paul Horgan, *Great River: The Rio Grande in North American History*
1956 Richard Hofstadter, *The Age of Reform*
1957 George F. Kennan, *Russia Leaves the War*
1958 Bray Hammond, *Banks and Politics in America From the Revolution to the Civil War*
1959 Leonard D. White and Jean Schneider, *The Republican Era; 1869-1901*
1960 Margaret Leech, *In the Days of McKinley*
1961 Herbert Feis, *Between War and Peace: The Potsdam Conference*
1962 Lawrence H. Gibson, *The Triumphant Empire: Thunderclouds Gather in the West*
1963 Constance McLaughlin Green, *Washington: Village and Capital, 1800-1878*
1964 Sumner Chilton Powell, *Puritan Village: The Formation of a New England Town*
1965 Irwin Unger, *The Greenback Era*
1966 Perry Miller, *Life of the Mind in America*
1967 William H. Goetzmann, *Exploration and Empire: The Explorer and Scientist in the Winning of the American West*
1968 Bernard Bailyn, *The Ideological Origins of the American Revolution*
1969 Leonard W. Levy, *Origin of the Fifth Amendment*
1970 Dean Acheson, *Present at the Creation: My Years in the State Department*
1971 James MacGregor Burns, *Roosevelt: The Soldier of Freedom*
1972 Carl N. Degler, *Neither Black nor White*
1973 Michael Kammen, *People of Paradox: An Inquiry Concerning the Origins of American Civilization*
1974 Daniel J. Boorstin, *The Americans: The Democratic Experience*
1975 Dumas Malone, *Jefferson and His Time*
1976 Paul Horgan, *Lamy of Santa Fe*
1977 David M. Potter, *The Impending Crisis*
1978 Alfred D. Chandler Jr., *The Visible Hand: The Managerial Revolution in American Business*
1979 Don E. Fehrenbacher, *The Dred Scott Case: Its Significance in American Law and Politics*
1980 Leon F. Litwack, *Been in the Storm So Long*
1981 Lawrence A. Cremin, *American Education: The National Experience, 1783-1876*
1982 C. Vann Woodward, ed., *Mary Chesnut's Civil War*
1983 Rhys L. Isaac, *The Transformation of Virginia, 1740-1790*

1985 Thomas K. McCraw, *Prophets of Regulation*
1986 Walter A. McDougall, *The Heavens and the Earth*
1987 Bernard Bailyn, *Voyagers to the West*
1988 Robert V. Bruce, *The Launching of Modern American Science, 1846-1876*
1989 Taylor Branch, *Parting the Waters: America in the King Years, 1954-63*; and James M. McPherson, *Battle Cry of Freedom: The Civil War Era*
1990 Stanley Karnow, *In Our Image: America's Empire in the Philippines*
1991 Laurel Thatcher Ulrich, *A Midwife's Tale: The Life of Martha Ballard,* based on her diary, 1785-1812
1992 Mark E. Neely Jr., *The Fate of Liberty: Abraham Lincoln and Civil Liberties*
1993 Gordon S. Wood, *The Radicalism of the American Revolution*
1995 Doris Kearns Goodwin, *No Ordinary Time: Franklin and Eleanor Roosevelt: The Home Front in World War II*
1996 Alan Taylor, *William Cooper's Town: Power and Persuasion on the Frontier of the Early American Republic*
1997 Jack N. Rakove, *Original Meanings: Politics and Ideas in the Making of the Constitution*
1998 Edward J. Larson, *Summer for the Gods: The Scopes Trial and America's Continuing Debate Over Science and Religion*
1999 Edwin G. Burrows and Mike Wallace, *Gotham: A History of New York City to 1898*
2000 David M. Kennedy, *Freedom From Fear: The American People in Depression and War, 1929-1945*
2001 Joseph J. Ellis, *Founding Brothers: The Revolutionary Generation*
2002 Louis Menand, *The Metaphysical Club: A Story of Ideas in America*
2003 Rick Atkinson, *An Army at Dawn: The War in North Africa, 1942-1943*
2004 Steven Hahn, *A Nation Under Our Feet: Black Political Struggles in the Rural South From Slavery to the Great Migration*
2005 David Hackett Fischer, *Washington's Crossing*

Biography or Autobiography

1917 Laura E. Richards and Maude Howe Elliott, assisted by Florence Howe Hall, *Julia Ward Howe*
1918 William Cabell Bruce, *Benjamin Franklin, Self-Revealed*
1919 Henry Adams, *The Education of Henry Adams*
1920 Albert J. Beveridge, *The Life of John Marshall*
1921 Edward Bok, *The Americanization of Edward Bok*
1922 Hamlin Garland, *A Daughter of the Middle Border*
1923 Burton J. Hendrick, *The Life and Letters of Walter H. Page*
1924 Michael Pupin, *From Immigrant to Inventor*
1925 M. A. DeWolfe Howe, *Barrett Wendell and His Letters*
1926 Harvey Cushing, *Life of Sir William Osler*
1927 Emory Holloway, *Whitman: An Interpretation in Narrative*
1928 Charles Edward Russell, *The American Orchestra and Theodore Thomas*

1929 Burton J. Hendrick, *The Training of an American: The Earlier Life and Letters of Walter H. Page*

1930 Marquis James, *The Raven* (Sam Houston)

1931 Henry James, *Charles W. Eliot*

1932 Henry F. Pringle, *Theodore Roosevelt*

1933 Allan Nevins, *Grover Cleveland*

1934 Tyler Dennett, *John Hay*

1935 Douglas Southall Freeman, *R. E. Lee*

1936 Ralph Barton Perry, *The Thought and Character of William James*

1937 Allan Nevins, *Hamilton Fish: The Inner History of the Grant Administration*

1938 Divided between Odell Shepard, *Pedlar's Progress* (Bronson Alcott) and Marquis James, *Andrew Jackson*

1939 Carl Van Doren, *Benjamin Franklin*

1940 Ray Stannard Baker, *Woodrow Wilson, Life and Letters*

1941 Ola Elizabeth Winslow, *Jonathan Edwards*

1942 Forrest Wilson, *Crusader in Crinoline* (Harriet Beecher Stowe)

1943 Samuel Eliot Morison, *Admiral of the Ocean Sea* (Christopher Columbus)

1944 Carleton Mabee, *The American Leonardo: The Life of Samuel F. B. Morse*

1945 Russell Blaine Nye, *George Bancroft: Brahmin Rebel*

1946 Linny Marsh Wolfe, *Son of the Wilderness* (John Muir)

1947 William Allen White, *Autobiography of William Allen White*

1948 Margaret Clapp, *Forgotten First Citizen: John Bigelow*

1949 Robert E. Sherwood, *Roosevelt and Hopkins*

1950 Samuel Flagg Bemis, *John Quincy Adams and the Foundations of American Foreign Policy*

1951 Margaret Louise Coit, *John C. Calhoun: American Portrait*

1952 Merlo J. Pusey, *Charles Evans Hughes*

1953 David J. Mays, *Edmund Pendleton, 1721-1803*

1954 Charles A. Lindbergh, *The Spirit of St. Louis*

1955 William S. White, *The Taft Story*

1956 Talbot F. Hamlin, *Benjamin Henry Latrobe*

1957 John F. Kennedy, *Profiles in Courage*

1958 Douglas Southall Freeman (Vols. I-VI) and John Alexander Carroll and Mary Wells Ashworth (Vol. VII), *George Washington*

1959 Arthur Walworth, *Woodrow Wilson: American Prophet*

1960 Samuel Eliot Morison, *John Paul Jones*

1961 David Donald, *Charles Sumner and the Coming of the Civil War*

1963 Leon Edel, *Henry James: Vols. 2-3*

1964 Walter Jackson Bate, *John Keats*

1965 Ernest Samuels, *Henry Adams*

1966 Arthur M. Schlesinger Jr., *A Thousand Days*

1967 Justin Kaplan, *Mr. Clemens and Mark Twain*

1968 George F. Kennan, *Memoirs (1925-1950)*

1969 B. L. Reid, *The Man From New York: John Quinn and His Friends*

1970 T. Harry Williams, *Huey Long*

1971 Lawrence Thompson, *Robert Frost: The Years of Triumph, 1915-1938*

1972 Joseph P. Lash, *Eleanor and Franklin*

1973 W. A. Swanberg, *Luce and His Empire*

1974 Louis Sheaffer, *O'Neill, Son and Artist*

1975 Robert A. Caro, *The Power Broker: Robert Moses and the Fall of New York*

1976 R.W.B. Lewis, *Edith Wharton: A Biography*

1977 John E. Mack, *A Prince of Our Disorder: The Life of T. E. Lawrence*

1978 Walter Jackson Bate, *Samuel Johnson*

1979 Leonard Baker, *Days of Sorrow and Pain: Leo Baeck and the Berlin Jews*

1980 Edmund Morris, *The Rise of Theodore Roosevelt*

1981 Robert K. Massie, *Peter the Great: His Life and World*

1982 William S. McFeely, *Grant: A Biography*

1983 Russell Baker, *Growing Up*

1984 Louis R. Harlan, *Booker T. Washington*

1985 Kenneth Silverman, *The Life and Times of Cotton Mather*

1986 Elizabeth Frank, *Louise Bogan: A Portrait*

1987 David J. Garrow, *Bearing the Cross: Martin Luther King Jr. and the Southern Christian Leadership Conference*

1988 David Herbert Donald, *Look Homeward: A Life of Thomas Wolfe*

1989 Richard Ellmann, *Oscar Wilde*

1990 Sebastian de Grazia, *Machiavelli in Hell*

1991 Steven Naifeh and Gregory White Smith, *Jackson Pollock: An American Saga*

1992 Lewis B. Puller Jr., *Fortunate Son: The Healing of a Vietnam Vet*

1993 David McCullough, *Truman*

1994 David Levering Lewis, *W.E.B. DuBois: Biography of a Race, 1868-1919*

1995 Joan D. Hedrick, *Harriet Beecher Stowe: A Life*

1996 Jack Miles, *God: A Biography*

1997 Frank McCourt, *Angela's Ashes: A Memoir*

1998 Katharine Graham, *Personal History*

1999 A. Scott Berg, *Lindbergh*

2000 Stacy Schiff, *Véra (Mrs. Vladimir Nabokov)*

2001 David Levering Lewis, *W.E.B. Du Bois: The Fight for Equality and the American Century, 1919-1963*

2002 David McCullough, *John Adams*

2003 Robert Caro, *The Years of Lyndon Johnson: Master of the Senate*

2004 William Taubman, *Khrushchev: The Man and His Era*

2005 Mark Stevens and Annalyn Swan, *de Kooning: An American Master*

Poetry

Before 1922, awards were funded by the Poetry Society.

1918 *Love Songs*, by Sara Teasdale

1919 *Old Road to Paradise*, by Margaret Widdemer; *Corn Huskers*, by Carl Sandburg

1922 Edwin Arlington Robinson, *Collected Poems*

1923 Edna St. Vincent Millay, *The Ballad of the Harp-Weaver; A Few Figs From Thistles; other works*

1924 Robert Frost, *New Hampshire: A Poem With Notes and Grace Notes*

1925 Edwin Arlington Robinson, *The Man Who Died Twice*
1926 Amy Lowell, *What's O'Clock*
1927 Leonora Speyer, *Fiddler's Farewell*
1928 Edwin Arlington Robinson, *Tristram*
1929 Stephen Vincent Benet, *John Brown's Body*
1930 Conrad Aiken, *Selected Poems*
1931 Robert Frost, *Collected Poems*
1932 George Dillon, *The Flowering Stone*
1933 Archibald MacLeish, *Conquistador*
1934 Robert Hillyer, *Collected Verse*
1935 Audrey Wurdemann, *Bright Ambush*
1936 Robert P. Tristram Coffin, *Strange Holiness*
1937 Robert Frost, *A Further Range*
1938 Marya Zaturenska, *Cold Morning Sky*
1939 John Gould Fletcher, *Selected Poems*
1940 Mark Van Doren, *Collected Poems*
1941 Leonard Bacon, *Sunderland Capture*
1942 William Rose Benet, *The Dust Which Is God*
1943 Robert Frost, *A Witness Tree*
1944 Stephen Vincent Benet, *Western Star*
1945 Karl Shapiro, *V-Letter and Other Poems*
1947 Robert Lowell, *Lord Weary's Castle*
1948 W. H. Auden, *The Age of Anxiety*
1949 Peter Viereck, *Terror and Decorum*
1950 Gwendolyn Brooks, *Annie Allen*
1951 Carl Sandburg, *Complete Poems*
1952 Marianne Moore, *Collected Poems*
1953 Archibald MacLeish, *Collected Poems*
1954 Theodore Roethke, *The Waking*
1955 Wallace Stevens, *Collected Poems*
1956 Elizabeth Bishop, *Poems, North and South*
1957 Richard Wilbur, *Things of This World*
1958 Robert Penn Warren, *Promises: Poems 1954-1956*
1959 Stanley Kunitz, *Selected Poems 1928-1958*
1960 W. D. Snodgrass, *Heart's Needle*
1961 Phyllis McGinley, *Times Three: Selected Verse From Three Decades*
1962 Alan Dugan, *Poems*
1963 William Carlos Williams, *Pictures From Breughel*
1964 Louis Simpson, *At the End of the Open Road*
1965 John Berryman, *77 Dream Songs*
1966 Richard Eberhart, *Selected Poems*
1967 Anne Sexton, *Live or Die*
1968 Anthony Hecht, *The Hard Hours*
1969 George Oppen, *Of Being Numerous*
1970 Richard Howard, *Untitled Subjects*
1971 William S. Merwin, *The Carrier of Ladders*
1972 James Wright, *Collected Poems*
1973 Maxine Winokur Kumin, *Up Country*
1974 Robert Lowell, *The Dolphin*
1975 Gary Snyder, *Turtle Island*

1976 John Ashbery, *Self-Portrait in a Convex Mirror*
1977 James Merrill, *Divine Comedies*
1978 Howard Nemerov, *Collected Poems*
1979 Robert Penn Warren, *Now and Then: Poems 1976-1978*
1980 Donald Justice, *Selected Poems*
1981 James Schuyler, *The Morning of the Poem*
1982 Sylvia Plath, *The Collected Poems*
1983 Galway Kinnell, *Selected Poems*
1984 Mary Oliver, *American Primitive*
1985 Carolyn Kizer, *Yin*
1986 Henry Taylor, *The Flying Change*
1987 Rita Dove, *Thomas and Beulah*
1988 William Meredith, *Partial Accounts: New and Selected Poems*
1989 Richard Wilbur, *New and Collected Poems*
1990 Charles Simic, *The World Doesn't End*
1991 Mona Van Duyn, *Near Changes*
1992 James Tate, *Selected Poems*
1993 Louise Glück, *The Wild Iris*
1994 Yusef Komunyakaa, *Neon Vernacular*
1995 Philip Levine, *The Simple Truth*
1996 Jorie Graham, *The Dream of the Unified Field*
1997 Lisel Mueller, *Alive Together: New and Selected Poems*
1998 Charles Wright, *Black Zodiac*
1999 Mark Strand, *Blizzard of One*
2000 C. K. Williams, *Repair*
2001 Stephen Dunn, *Different Hours*
2002 Carl Dennis, *Practical Gods*
2003 Paul Muldoon, *Moy Sand and Gravel*
2004 Franz Wright, *Walking to Martha's Vineyard*
2005 Ted Kooser, *Delights & Shadows*

General Nonfiction

1962 Theodore H. White, *The Making of the President 1960*
1963 Barbara W. Tuchman, *The Guns of August*
1964 Richard Hofstadter, *Anti-Intellectualism in American Life*
1965 Howard Mumford Jones, *O Strange New World*
1966 Edwin Way Teale, *Wandering Through Winter*
1967 David Brion Davis, *The Problem of Slavery in Western Culture*
1968 Will and Ariel Durant, *Rousseau and Revolution*
1969 Norman Mailer, *The Armies of the Night;* Rene Jules Dubos, *So Human an Animal: How We Are Shaped by Surroundings and Events*
1970 Eric H. Erikson, *Gandhi's Truth*
1971 John Toland, *The Rising Sun*
1972 Barbara W. Tuchman, *Stilwell and the American Experience in China, 1911-1945*
1973 Frances FitzGerald, *Fire in the Lake: The Vietnamese and the Americans in Vietnam;* Robert Coles, *Children of Crisis,* Volumes II & III
1974 Ernest Becker, *The Denial of Death*
1975 Annie Dillard, *Pilgrim at Tinker Creek*
1976 Robert N. Butler, *Why Survive? Being Old in America*
1977 William W. Warner, *Beautiful Swimmers*
1978 Carl Sagan, *The Dragons of Eden*

1979 Edward O. Wilson, *On Human Nature*

1980 Douglas R. Hofstadter, *Gödel, Escher, Bach: An Eternal Golden Braid*

1981 Carl E. Schorske, *Fin-de-Siècle Vienna: Politics and Culture*

1982 Tracy Kidder, *The Soul of a New Machine*

1983 Susan Sheehan, *Is There No Place on Earth for Me?*

1984 Paul Starr, *Social Transformation of American Medicine*

1985 Studs Terkel, *The Good War*

1986 Joseph Lelyveld, *Move Your Shadow;* J. Anthony Lukas, *Common Ground*

1987 David K. Shipler, *Arab and Jew*

1988 Richard Rhodes, *The Making of the Atomic Bomb*

1989 Neil Sheehan, *A Bright Shining Lie: John Paul Vann and America in Vietnam*

1990 Dale Maharidge and Michael Williamson, *And Their Children After Them*

1991 Bert Holldobler and Edward O. Wilson, *The Ants*

1992 Daniel Yergin, *The Prize: The Epic Quest for Oil*

1993 Garry Wills, *Lincoln at Gettysburg*

1994 David Remnick, *Lenin's Tomb: The Last Days of the Soviet Empire*

1995 Jonathan Weiner, *The Beak of the Finch: A Story of Evolution in Our Time*

1996 Tina Rosenberg, *The Haunted Land: Facing Europe's Ghosts After Communism*

1997 Richard Kluger, *Ashes to Ashes: America's Hundred-Year Cigarette War, the Public Health, and the Unabashed Triumph of Philip Morris*

1998 Jared Diamond, *Guns, Germs, and Steel: The Fates of Human Societies*

1999 John McPhee, *Annals of the Former World*

2000 John W. Dower, *Embracing Defeat: Japan in the Wake of World War II*

2001 Herbert P. Bix, *Hirohito and the Making of Modern Japan*

2002 Diane McWhorter, *Carry Me Home: Birmingham, Alabama: the Climactic Battle of the Civil Rights Revolution*

2003 Samantha Power, *A Problem From Hell: America and the Age of Genocide*

2004 Anne Applebaum, *Gulag: A History*

2005 Steve Coll, *Ghost Wars*

Special Citation in Letters

1944 Richard Rodgers and Oscar Hammerstein II, for *Oklahoma!*

1957 Kenneth Roberts, for his historical novels

1960 *The Armada*, by Garrett Mattingly

1961 *American Heritage Picture History of the Civil War*

1973 *George Washington, Vols. I-IV*, by James Thomas Flexner

1977 Alex Haley, for *Roots*

1978 E.B. White

1984 Theodore Seuss Geisel (Dr. Seuss)

1992 Art Spiegelman, for *Maus*

National Book Awards, 1950-2004

The National Book Awards (known as the American Book Awards from 1980 to 1986) are administered by the National Book Foundation and have been given annually since 1950. The prizes, each valued at $10,000, are awarded to U.S. citizens for works published in the U.S. in the 12 months prior to the nominations. In some years, multiple awards were given for nonfiction in various categories; in such cases, the history and biography (if any) or biography winner is listed. Nonfiction winners in certain separate categories may not be shown.

Fiction

Year Author, Title
1950 Nelson Algren, *The Man With the Golden Arm*
1951 William Faulkner, *The Collected Stories*
1952 James Jones, *From Here to Eternity*
1953 Ralph Ellison, *Invisible Man*
1954 Saul Bellow, *The Adventures of Augie March*
1955 William Faulkner, *A Fable*
1956 John O'Hara, *Ten North Frederick*
1957 Wright Morris, *The Field of Vision*
1958 John Cheever, *The Wapshot Chronicle*
1959 Bernard Malamud, *The Magic Barrel*
1960 Philip Roth, *Goodbye, Columbus*
1961 Conrad Richter, *The Waters of Kronos*
1962 Walker Percy, *The Moviegoer*
1963 J.F. Powers, *Morte d'Urban*
1964 John Updike, *The Centaur*
1965 Saul Bellow, *Herzog*
1966 Katherine Anne Porter, *The Collected Stories*
1967 Bernard Malamud, *The Fixer*
1968 Thornton Wilder, *The Eighth Day*
1969 Jerzy Kosinski, *Steps*
1970 Joyce Carol Oates, *Them*
1971 Saul Bellow, *Mr. Sammler's Planet*
1972 Flannery O'Connor, *The Complete Stories*
1973 John Barth, *Chimera*
1974 Thomas Pynchon, *Gravity's Rainbow*
     Isaac Bashevis Singer, *A Crown of Feathers*
1975 Robert Stone, *Dog Soldiers*
1976 William Gaddis, *JR*
1977 Wallace Stegner, *The Spectator Bird*
1978 Mary Lee Settle, *Blood Ties*
1979 Tim O'Brien, *Going After Cacciato*
1980 William Styron, *Sophie's Choice*
1981 Wright Morris, *Plains Song*
1982 John Updike, *Rabbit Is Rich*
1983 Alice Walker, *The Color Purple*
1984 Ellen Gilchrist, *Victory Over Japan*
1985 Don DeLillo, *White Noise*

Year Author, Title

1986 E.L. Doctorow, *World's Fair*
1987 Larry Heinemann, *Paco's Story*
1988 Pete Dexter, *Paris Trout*
1989 John Casey, *Spartina*
1990 Charles Johnson, *Middle Passage*
1991 Norman Rush, *Mating*
1992 Cormac McCarthy, *All the Pretty Horses*
1993 E. Annie Proulx, *The Shipping News*
1994 William Gaddis, *A Frolic of His Own*
1995 Philip Roth, *Sabbath's Theater*
1996 Andrea Barrett, *Ship Fever and Other Stories*
1997 Charles Frazier, *Cold Mounatin*
1998 Alice McDermott, *Charming Billy*
1999 Ha Jin, *Waiting*
2000 Susan Sontag, *In America*
2001 Jonathan Franzen, *The Corrections*
2002 Julia Glass, *Three Junes*
2003 Shirley Hazzard, *The Great Fire*
2004 Lily Tuck, *The News from Paraguay*

Nonfiction

Year Author, Title

1950 Ralph L. Rusk, *Ralph Waldo Emerson*
1951 Newton Arvin, *Herman Melville*
1952 Rachel Carson, *The Sea Around Us*
1953 Bernard A. De Voto, *The Course of an Empire*
1954 Bruce Catton, *A Stillness at Appomattox*
1955 Joseph Wood Krutch, *The Measure of Man*
1956 Herbert Kubly, *An American in Italy*
1957 George F. Kennan, *Russia Leaves the War*
1958 Catherine Drinker Bowen, *The Lion and the Throne*
1959 J. Christopher Herold, *Mistress to an Age: A Life of Madame De Stael*
1960 Richard Ellman, *James Joyce*
1961 William L. Shirer, *The Rise and Fall of the Third Reich*
1962 Lewis Mumford, *The City in History: Its Origins, Its Transformations, and Its Prospects*
1963 Leon Edel, *Henry James: Vol. II: The Conquest of London; Vol. III: The Middle Years*
1964 Wllliam H. McNeill, *The Rise of the West: A History of the Human Community*
1965 Louis Fisher, *The Life of Lenin*
1966 Arthur M. Schlesinger, Jr., *A Thousand Days: John F. Kennedy in the White House*
1967 Peter Gay, *The Enlightenment, An Interpretation Vol I: The Rise of Modern Paganism*
1968 George F. Kennan, *Memoirs: 1925–1950*
1969 Winthrop D. Jordan, *White Over Black: American Attitudes Toward the Negro, 1550-1812*
1970 T. Harry Williams, *Huey Long*

Year Author, Title

1971 James MacGregor Burns, *Roosevelt: The Soldier of Freedom*

1972 Joseph P. Lash, *Eleanor and Franklin: The Story of Their Relationship, Based on Eleanor Roosevelt's Private Papers*

1973 James Thomas Flexner, *George Washington, Vol. IV: Anguish and Farewell, 1793-1799*

1974 John Clive, *Macaulay, The Shaping of the Historian*; Douglas Day, *Malcolm Lowry: A Biography*

1975 Richard B. Sewall, *The Life of Emily Dickinson*

1976 David Brion Davis, *The Problem of Slavery in the Age of Revolution, 1770-1823*

1977 W.A. Swanberg, *Norman Thomas: The Last Idealist*

1978 W. Jackson Bate, *Samuel Johnson*

1979 Arthur M. Schlesinger, Jr., *Robert Kennedy and His Times*

1980 Tom Wolfe, *The Right Stuff*

1981 Maxine Hong Kingston, *China Men*

1982 Tracy Kidder, *The Soul of a New Machine*

1983 Fox Butterfield, *China: Alive in the Bitter Sea*

1984 Robert V. Remini, *Andrew Jackson and the Course of American Democracy, 1833-1845*

1985 J. Anthony Lukas, *Common Ground: A Turbulent Decade in the Lives of Three American Families*

1986 Barry Lopez, *Arctic Dreams*

1987 Richard Rhodes, *The Making of the Atom Bomb*

1988 Neil Sheehan, *A Bright Shining Lie: John Paul Vann and America in Vietnam*

1989 Thomas L. Friedman, *From Beirut to Jerusalem*

1990 Ron Chernow, *The House of Morgan: An American Banking Dynasty and the Rise of Modern Finance*

1991 Orlando Patterson, *Freedom*

1992 Paul Monette, *Becoming a Man: Half a Life Story*

1993 Gore Vidal, *United States: Essays 1952-1992*

1994 Sherwin B. Nuland, *How We Die: Reflections on Life's Final Chapter*

1995 Tina Rosenberg, *The Haunted Land: Facing Europe's Ghosts After Communism*

1996 James Carroll, *An American Requiem: God, My Father, and the War That Came Between Us*

1997 Joseph J. Ellis, *American Sphinx: The Character of Thomas Jefferson*

1998 Edward Ball, *Slaves in the Family*

1999 John W. Dower, *Embracing Defeat: Japan in the Wake of World War II*

2000 Nathaniel Philbrick, *In the Heart of the Sea: The Tragedy of the Whaleship Essex*

2001 Andrew Solomon, *The Noonday Demon: An Atlas of Depression*

2002 Robert A. Caro, *Master of the Senate: The Years of Lyndon Johnson*

2003 Carlos Eire, *Waiting for Snow in Havana: Confessions of a Cuban Boy*

2004 Kevin Boyle, *Arc of Justice: A Saga of Race, Civil Rights, and Murder in the Jazz Age*

The Man Booker Prize for Fiction, 1969-2004

The Booker Prize for fiction, established in 1968, is awarded annually in October for what is judged the best full-length novel written in English by a citizen of the UK, the Commonwealth, or the Irish Republic. In 2002 sponsorship of the award was taken over by Man Group PLC, the name was changed to the Man Booker Prize, and the amount was increased from £20,000 to £50,000. The prize money for being named to the shortlist of 6 was also increased from £1,000 to £2,500.

Year   Author, Title

1969 P. H. Newby, *Something to Answer For*
1970 Bernice Rubens, *The Elected Member*
1971 V. S. Naipaul, *In a Free State*
1972 John Berger, *G*
1973 J. G. Farrell, *The Siege of Krishnapur*
1974 Nadine Gordimer, *The Conservationist; Stanley Middleton, Holiday*
1975 Ruth Prawer Jhabvala, *Heat & Dust*
1976 David Storey, *Saville*
1977 Paul Scott, *Staying On*
1978 Iris Murdoch, *The Sea, The Sea*
1979 Penelope Fitzgerald, *Offshore*
1980 William Golding, *Rites of Passage*
1981 Salman Rushdie, *Midnight's Children*
1982 Thomas Keneally, *Schindler's Ark*
1983 J. M. Coetzee, *Life and Times of Michael K*
1984 Anita Brookner, *Hotel du Lac*
1985 Keri Hulme, *The Bone People*
1986 Kingsley Amis, *The Old Devils*
1987 Penelope Lively, *Moon Tiger*
1988 Peter Carey, *Oscar and Lucinda*
1989 Kazuo Ishiguro, *The Remains of the Day*
1990 A. S. Byatt, *Possession*
1991 Ben Okri, *The Famished Road*
1992 Michael Ondaatje, *The English Patient;*
     Barry Unsworth, *Sacred Hunger*
1993 Roddy Doyle, *Paddy Clarke Ha Ha Ha*
1994 James Kelman, *How Late It Was, How Late*
1995 Pat Barker, *The Ghost Road*
1996 Graham Swift, *Last Orders*
1997 Arundhati Roy, *The God of Small Things*
1998 Ian McEwan, *Amsterdam*
1999 J. M. Coetzee, *Disgrace*
2000 Margaret Atwood, *The Blind Assassin*
2001 Peter Carey, *True History of the Kelly Gang*
2002 Yann Martel, *Life of Pi*
2003 DBC Pierre, *Vernon God Little*
2004 Alan Hollinghurst, *The Line of Beauty*

Newbery Medal Books, 1922-2005

The Newbery Medal is awarded annually by the Association for Library Service to Children, a division of the American Library Association, to the author of the most distinguished contribution to American literature for children.

Year Book, Author

1922 *The Story of Mankind,* Hendrik Willem van Loon
1923 *The Voyages of Dr. Dolittle,* Hugh Lofting
1924 *The Dark Frigate,* Charles Boardman Hawes
1925 *Tales From Silver Lands,* Charles Joseph Finger
1926 *Shen of the Sea,* Arthur Bowie Chrisman
1927 *Smoky, the Cowhorse,* Will James
1928 *Gay-Neck,* Dhan Gopal Mukerji
1929 *The Trumpeter of Krakow,* Eric P. Kelly
1930 *Hitty, Her First Hundred Years,* Rachel Field
1931 *The Cat Who Went to Heaven,* Elizabeth Coatsworth
1932 *Waterless Mountain,* Laura Adams Armer
1933 *Young Fu of the Upper Yangtze,* Elizabeth Foreman Lewis
1934 *Invincible Louisa,* Cornelia Lynde Meigs
1935 *Dobry,* Monica Shannon
1936 *Caddie Woodlawn,* Carol Ryrie Brink
1937 *Roller Skates,* Ruth Sawyer
1938 *The White Stag,* Kate Seredy
1939 *Thimble Summer,* Elizabeth Enright
1940 *Daniel Boone,* James Daugherty
1941 *Call It Courage,* Armstrong Sperry
1942 *The Matchlock Gun,* Walter D. Edmonds
1943 *Adam of the Road,* Elizabeth Janet Gray
1944 *Johnny Tremain,* Esther Forbes
1945 *Rabbit Hill,* Robert Lawson
1946 *Strawberry Girl,* Lois Lenski
1947 *Miss Hickory,* Carolyn S. Bailey
1948 *Twenty-One Balloons,* William Pène Du Bois
1949 *King of the Wind,* Marguerite Henry
1950 *The Door in the Wall,* Marguerite de Angeli
1951 *Amos Fortune, Free Man,* Elizabeth Yates
1952 *Ginger Pye,* Eleanor Estes
1953 *Secret of the Andes,* Ann Nolan Clark
1954 *. . . And Now Miguel,* Joseph Krumgold
1955 *The Wheel on the School,* Meindert DeJong
1956 *Carry On, Mr. Bowditch,* Jean Lee Latham
1957 *Miracles on Maple Hill,* Virginia Sorensen
1958 *Rifles for Watie,* Harold Keith
1959 *The Witch of Blackbird Pond,* Elizabeth George Speare
1960 *Onion John,* Joseph Krumgold
1961 *Island of the Blue Dolphins,* Scott O'Dell
1962 *The Bronze Bow,* Elizabeth George Speare

Year Book, Author

1963 *A Wrinkle in Time,* Madeleine L'Engle
1964 *It's Like This, Cat,* Emily Cheney Neville
1965 *Shadow of a Bull,* Maja Wojciechowska
1966 *I, Juan de Pareja,* Elizabeth Borton de Trevino
1967 *Up a Road Slowly,* Irene Hunt
1968 *From the Mixed-Up Files of Mrs. Basil E. Frankweiler,* E. L. Konigsburg
1969 *The High King,* Lloyd Alexander
1970 *Sounder,* William H. Armstrong
1971 *The Summer of the Swans,* Betsy Byars
1972 *Mrs. Frisby and the Rats of NIMH,* Robert C. O'Brien
1973 *Julie of the Wolves,* Jean George
1974 *The Slave Dancer,* Paula Fox
1975 *M. C. Higgins the Great,* Virginia Hamilton
1976 *Grey King,* Susan Cooper
1977 *Roll of Thunder, Hear My Cry,* Mildred D. Taylor
1978 *Bridge to Terabithia,* Katherine Paterson
1979 *The Westing Game,* Ellen Raskin
1980 *A Gathering of Days,* Joan Blos
1981 *Jacob Have I Loved,* Katherine Paterson
1982 *A Visit to William Blake's Inn: Poems for Innocent and Experienced Travelers,* Nancy Willard
1983 *Dicey's Song,* Cynthia Voigt
1984 *Dear Mr. Henshaw,* Beverly Cleary
1985 *The Hero and the Crown,* Robin McKinley
1986 *Sarah, Plain and Tall,* Patricia MacLachlan
1987 *The Whipping Boy,* Sid Fleischman
1988 *Lincoln: A Photobiography,* Russell Freedman
1989 *Joyful Noise: Poems for Two Voices,* Paul Fleischman
1990 *Number the Stars,* Lois Lowry
1991 *Maniac Magee,* Jerry Spinelli
1992 *Shiloh,* Phyllis Reynolds Naylor
1993 *Missing May,* Cynthia Rylant
1994 *The Giver,* Lois Lowry
1995 *Walk Two Moons,* Sharon Creech
1996 *The Midwife's Apprentice,* Karen Cushman
1997 *The View From Saturday,* E. L. Konigsburg
1998 *Out of the Dust,* Karen Hesse
1999 *Holes,* Louis Sachar
2000 *Bud, Not Buddy,* Christopher Paul Curtis
2001 *A Year Down Yonder,* Richard Peck
2002 *A Single Shard,* Linda Sue Park
2003 *Crispin: The Cross of Lead,* Avi
2004 *The Tale of Despereaux: Being the Story of a Mouse, a Princess, Some Soup, and a Spool of Thread,* by Kate DiCamillo, illustrated by Timothy Basil Ering
2005 *Kira-Kira,* by Cynthia Kadohata

Caldecott Medal Books, 1938-2005

The Caldecott Medal is awarded annually by the Association for Library Service to Children, a division of the American Library Association, to the illustrator of the most distinguished American picture book for children.

Year Book, Illustrator

1938 *Animals of the Bible*, Dorothy P. Lathrop
1939 *Mei Li*, Thomas Handforth
1940 *Abraham Lincoln*, Ingri & Edgar Parin d'Aulaire
1941 *They Were Strong and Good*, Robert Lawson
1942 *Make Way for Ducklings*, Robert McCloskey
1943 *The Little House*, Virginia Lee Burton
1944 *Many Moons*, Louis Slobodkin
1945 *Prayer for a Child*, Elizabeth Orton Jones
1946 *The Rooster Crows*, Maude & Miska Petersham
1947 *The Little Island*, Leonard Weisgard
1948 *White Snow, Bright Snow*, Roger Duvoisin
1949 *The Big Snow*, Berta & Elmer Hader
1950 *Song of the Swallows*, Leo Politi
1951 *The Egg Tree*, Karherine Milhous
1952 *Finders Keepers*, Nicolas, pseud. (Nicholas Mordvinoff)
1953 *The Biggest Bear*, Lynd Ward
1954 *Madeline's Rescue*, Ludwig Bemelmans
1955 *Cinderella, or the Little Glass Slipper*, Marcia Brown
1956 *Frog Went A-Courtin'*, Feodor Rojankovsky
1957 *A Tree Is Nice*, Marc Simont
1958 *Time of Wonder*, Robert McCloskey
1959 *Chanticleer and the Fox,* Barbara Cooney
1960 *Nine Days to Christmas*, Marie Hall Ets
1961 *Baboushka and the Three Kings*, Nicolas Sidjakov
1962 *Once a Mouse*, Marcia Brown
1963 *The Snowy Day*, Ezra Jack Keats
1964 *Where the Wild Things Are*, Maurice Sendak
1965 *May I Bring a Friend?*, Beni Montresor
1966 *Always Room for One More*, Nonny Hogrogian
1967 *Sam, Bang, and Moonshine*, Evaline Ness
1968 *Drummer Hoff*, Ed Emberley
1969 *The Fool of the World and the Flying Ship*, Uri Shulevitz
1970 *Sylvester and the Magic Pebble*, William Steig
1971 *A Story A Story,* Gail E. Haley
1972 *One Fine Day*, Nonny Hogrogian
1973 *The Funny Little Woman*, Blair Lent
1974 *Duffy and the Devil*, Margot Zemach
1975 *Arrow to the Sun*, Gerald McDermott
1976 *Why Mosquitoes Buzz in People's Ears*, Leo & Diane Dillon
1977 *Ashanti to Zulu: African Traditions*, Leo & Diane Dillon
1978 *Noah's Ark*, Peter Spier
1979 *The Girl Who Loved Wild Horses*, Paul Goble
1980 *Ox-Cart Man*, Barbara Cooney
1981 *Fables*, Arnold Lobel

Year Book, Illustrator
1982 *Jumanji*, Chris Van Allsburg
1983 *Shadow*, Marcia Brown
1984 *The Glorious Flight: Across the Channel with Louis Bleriot*, Alice and Martin Provensen
1985 *Saint George and the Dragon*, Trina Schart Hyman
1986 *The Polar Express*, Chris Van Allsburg
1987 *Hey, Al*, Richard Egielski
1988 *Owl Moon*, John Schoenherr
1989 *Song and Dance Man*, Stephen Grammell
1990 *Lon Po Po: A Red-Riding Hood Story From China*, Ed Young
1991 *Black and White*, David Macaulay
1992 *Tuesday*, David Wiesner
1993 *Mirette on the High Wire*, Emily Arnold McCully
1994 *Grandfather's Journey*, Allen Say
1995 *Smoky Night*, David Diaz
1996 *Officer Buckle and Gloria*, Peggy Rathmann
1997 *Golem*, David Wisniewski
1998 *Rapunzel*, Paul O. Zelinsky
1999 *Snowflake Bentley*, Mary Azarian
2000 *Joseph Had a Little Overcoat*, Simms Taback
2001 *So You Want to be President?*, David Small
2002 *The Three Pigs*, David Wiesner
2003 *My Friend Rabbit*, Eric Rohmann
2004 *The Man Who Walked Between the Towers*, Mordicai Gerstein
2005 *Kitten's First Full Moon*, Kevin Henkes

Miscellaneous Book Awards

(Awarded in 2004, unless otherwise noted)

Academy of American Poets Awards. Academy Fellowship, $25,000 stipend: Jane Hirshfield. James Laughlin Award, $5,000: Jeff Clark, *Music and Suicide*. Walt Whitman Award, $5,000: Geri Doran, *Resin*. Harold Morton Landon Translation Award, $1,000: Charles Martin, *Metamorphoses*; Anselm Hollo, *Pentii Saarikoski's Trilogy*. Lenore Marshall Poetry Prize, $25,000: Donald Revell, *My Mojave*. Raiziss/de Palchi Translation Award (fellowship), $20,000: Ann Snodgrass, *Selected Poems of Vittorio Sereni*. Wallace Stevens Award, for mastery in the art of poetry, $100,000: Mark Strand.

American Academy of Arts and Letters. Academy Awards in Literature ($7,500 each): Henri Cole, Marilyn Hacker, Samuel Hynes, Arnost Lustig, Joe Ashby Porter, Louis D. Rubin, Paula Vogel, Greg Williamson. Michael Braude Award for Light Verse, $5,000: R.S. Gwynn. Benjamin H. Danks Award, $20,000: Doug Wright. E. M. Forster Award, $15,000: Robin Robertson. Sue Kaufman Prize for First Fiction, $2,500: Nell Freudenberger, *Lucky Girls*. Award of Merit for Poetry, $10,000: Rosanna Warren. Katherine Anne Porter Award, $20,000: Nicholson Baker. Richard and Hinda Rosenthal Foundation Award, $5,000: Olympia Vernon, *Eden*. Harold D. Vursell Memorial Award,

$10,000: Judith Thurman. Morton Dawen Zabel Award, $10,000: Leonard Barkan. Rome Fellowships in Literature, one-year residence at the American Academy in Rome, for 2004-2005: Anthony Doerr (writer), Lisa Williams (poet).

Bollingen Prize in Poetry, by the Yale Univ. Library (2005): Jay Wright

Edgar Awards, by the Mystery Writers of America: Grand Master award: Joseph Wambaugh. Best novel: *Resurrection Men,* Ian Rankin. Best first novel by an American author: *Death of a Nationalist,* Rebecca Pawel. Best paperback original: *Find Me Again,* Sylvia Maultash Warsh. Best Critical/Biographical: *Beautiful Shadow: A Life of Patricia Highsmith,* Andrew Wilson.

Golden Kite Awards, by Society of Children's Book Writers and Illustrators. Fiction: Jerry Spinelli, *Milkweed.* Nonfiction: Robert Byrd, *Leonardo: Beautiful Dreamer.* Picture-illustration: Loren Long, *I Dream of Trains* (Angela Johnson, author). Picture book text: Amy Timberlake, *The Dirty Cowboy* (Adam Rex, illus.)

Le Prix Goncourt, by Académie Goncourt: Laurent Gaudé, *Le Soleil des Scorta* (The Sun of the Scortas)

Hugo Awards, by the World Science Fiction Convention. Novel: *Paladin of Souls,* Lois McMaster Bujold. Novella: *The Cookie Monster,* Vernor Vinge. Novelette: *Legions in Time,* Michael Swanwick. Short story: "A Study in Emerald," Neil Gaiman. John W. Campbell Award for Best New Writer: Jay Lake.

Coretta Scott King Award, by American Library Assn., for African American authors and illustrators of outstanding books for children and young adults. Author: Toni Morrison, *Remember: The Journey to School Integration.* Illustrator: Kadir Nelson, *Ellington Was Not a Street* (Ntozake Shange, author).

Lincoln Prize, by Lincoln and Soldiers Institute at Gettysburg College, for contribution to Civil War studies, $35,000 and bust of Lincoln (2005): Allen C. Guelzo, *Lincoln's Emancipation Proclamation: The End of Slavery in America.* 2nd place, $15,000: Harold Holzer, *Lincoln at Cooper Union.*

National Book Critics Circle Awards. Fiction: Edward P. Jones, *The Known World.* Nonfiction: Paul Hendrickson, *Sons of Mississippi.* Criticism: Rebecca Solnit, *River of Shadows: Eadweard Muybridge and the Technological Wild West.* Biography/Autobiography: William Taubman, *Khrushchev: The Man and His Era.* Poetry: Susan Stewart, *Columbarium.* Nona Balakian Citation for Excellence in Reviewing: Scott McLemee. Ivan Sandrof Lifetime Achievement Award: Studs Terkel.

Nebula Awards, by the Science Fiction Writers of America. Novel: *The Speed of Dark,* Elizabeth Moon. Novella: *Coraline,* Neil Gaiman. Novelette: *The Empire of Ice Cream,* Jeffrey Ford. Short story: "What I Didn't See," Karen Joy Fowler.

PEN/Faulkner Award, for fiction, $15,000: John Updike, *The Early Stories.*

Whitbread Book of the Year Award, by Whitbread PLC: £25,000: (2005): Andrea Levy, *Small Island.*

ALA Notable New Books, 2004

Source: List published by American Library Association, Chicago, IL, 2005, for books published in 2004.

Fiction

The Lemon Table: Stories, Julian Barnes
The Half Brother, Lars Saabye Christensen
Birds Without Wings, Louis de Bernieres
I Sailed with Magellan, Stuart Dybek
The Swallows of Kabul, Yasmina Khadra
The Madonna of Excelsior, Zakes Mda
Cloud Atlas, David Mitchell
Runaway: Stories, Alice Munro
Popular Music from Vittula, Mikael Niemi
The Plot Against America, Philip Roth
Old School, Tobias Wolff

Nonfiction

Alexander Hamilton, Ron Chernow
One With Nineveh: Politics, Consumption, and the Human Future, Paul R. and Anne H. Ehrlich
Washington's Crossing (Pivotal Moments in American History), David Hackett Fischer
Pandora's Baby: How the First Test Tube Babies Sparked the Reproductive Revolution, Robin Marantz Henig
Chain of Command: The Road from 9/11 to Abu Ghraib, Seymour M. Hersh
Goya, Robert Hughes
The Year That Rocked the World, Mark Kurlansky
Outwitting History: The Amazing Adventures of a Man Who Rescued a Million Yiddish Books, Aaron Lansky
Civil Wars: A Battle for Gay Marriage, David Moats
The 9/11 Commission Report, National Commission on Terrorist Attacks
Sea of Glory: America's Voyage of Discovery, the U.S. Exploring Expedition, 1838-1842, Nathaniel Philbrick
The Ticket Out: Darryl Strawberry and the Boys of Crenshaw, Michael Sokolove
One Man's Castle: Clarence Darrow in Defense of the American Dream, Phyllis Vine

Poetry

The Collected Poetry of Nikki Giovanni: 1968-1998, Nikki Giovanni
Delights & Shadows, Ted Kooser

Young Adults

The Garden, Elsie V. Aidinoff
George Washington, Spymaster, Thomas B. Allen
Fire-Eaters, David Almond

Sign of the Qin: Outlaws of Moonshadow Marsh, No. 1, L.G. Bass

With Courage and Cloth: Winning the Fight for a Woman's Right to Vote, Ann Bausum

Wake Up Our Souls: A Celebration of Black American Artists, Tonya Bolden

The Unthinkable Thoughts of Jacob Green, Joshua Braff

Doing It, Melvin Burgess

Al Capone Does My Shirts, Gennifer Choldenko

Daniel Half Human and the Good Nazi, David Chotjewitz

Splintering, Eireann Corrigan

Bucking the Sarge, Christopher Paul Curtis

The Blue Girl, Charles de Lint

Dr. Ernest Drake's Dragonology, ed. Dugald Steer

The Hollow Kingdom, Clare B. Dunkle

The Sea of Trolls, Nancy Farmer

The Oracle Betrayed, Catherine Fisher

Who Am I Without Him?: Stories About Girls and the Boys in Their Lives, Sharon Flake

Nothing to Lose, Alex Flinn

The Voice That Challenged a Nation: Marian Anderson and the Struggle for Equal Rights, Russell Freedman

Tending to Grace, Kimberly Newton Fusco

Gothic: Ten Dark Original Tales, Deborah Noyes

Andy Warhol: Prince of Pop, Jan Greenberg and Sandra Jordan

Donorboy, Brendan Halpin

Godless, Pete Hautman

The Race to Save the Lord God Bird, Phillip M. Hoose

Eagle Strike: An Alex Rider Adventure, Anthony Horowitz

Worlds Afire: The Hartford Circus Fire of 1944, Paul B. Janeczko

Mable Riley: A Reliable Record of Humdrum, Peril, and Romance, Marthe Jocelyn

Bird, Angela Johnson

A Fast and Brutal Wing, Kathleen Jeffrie Johnson

The Key to the Golden Firebird, Maureen Johnson

Margaux With an X, Ron Koertge

The Blue Mirror, Kathe Koja

The Outcasts of 19 Schuyler Place, E.L. Konigsburg

Yossel, April 19, 1943: A Story of the Warsaw Ghetto Uprising, Joe Kubert

A Crack in the Line, Michael Lawrence

B for Buster, Iain Lawrence

Heck, Superhero, Martine Leavitt

The Realm of Possibility, David Levithan

Saving Francesca, Melina Marchetta

Sunshine, Robin McKinley

An Earthly Knight, Janet McNaughton

A Dream of Freedom: The Civil Rights Movement from 1954 to 1968, Diane McWhorter

Curse of the Blue Tattoo: Being an Account of the Misadventures of Jacky Faber, Midshipman and Fine Lady, L.A. Meyer

Fleshmarket, Nicola Morgan

The Year of Secret Assignments, Jaclyn Moriarty

Private Peaceful, Michael Morpurgo

Here in Harlem: Poems in Many Voices, Walter Dean Myers

Bound, Donna Jo Napoli

Rock Star, Superstar, Blake Nelson

Airborn, Kenneth Oppel

The Teacher's Funeral: A Comedy in Three Parts, Richard Peck

Luna: A Novel, Julie Anne Peters

A Hat Full of Sky, Terry Pratchett

Under the Wolf, Under the Dog, Adam Rapp

Predator's Gold, Philip Reeve

Promises to Keep: How Jackie Robinson Changed America, Sharon Robinson

how i live now, Meg Rosoff

Sammy and Juliana in Hollywood, Benjamin Alire Saenz

Persepolis 2: The Story of a Return, Marjane Satrapi

Lizzie Bright and the Buckminster Boy, Gary D. Schmidt

It's a Bird, Steven T. Seagle

The Safe-Keeper's Secret, Sharon Shinn

The Schwa Was Here, Neal Shusterman

The Radioactive Boy Scout: The True Story of a Boy and His Backyard Nuclear Reactor, Ken Silverstein

One of Those Hideous Books where the Mother Dies, Sonya Sones

Can't Get There from Here, Todd Strasser

Chanda's Secrets, Allan Stratton

The Golem's Eye: The Bartimaeus Trilogy, Book Two, Jonathan Stroud

Chief Sunrise, John McGraw, and Me, Timothy Tocher

Sky: A Novel in 3 Sets and an Encore, Roderick Townley

No Shame, No Fear, Ann Turnbull

Working Fire: The Making of an Accidental Fireman, Zac Unger

Montmorency: Thief, Liar, Gentleman?, Eleanor Updale

D-Day: The Greatest Invasion, Dan van der Vat

So B. It: A Novel, Sarah Weeks

Double Helix, Nancy Werlin

So Yesterday, Scott Westerfield

Fray, Joss Whedon

See You Down the Road, Kim Ablon Whitney

No Laughter Here, Rita Williams-Garcia

New Found Land: Lewis and Clark's Voyage of Discovery, Allan Wolf

The Haunting of Alaizabel Cray, Chris Wooding

Behind You, Jacqueline Woodson

Prince Across the Water, Jane Yolen and Robert J. Harris

Some Notable New Books for Children, 2004

Source: List published by American Library Association, Chicago, IL, 2005, for books published in 2004.

Younger Readers

Home, Jeannie Baker
Baby Danced the Polka, Karen Beaumont
Odd Boy Out: Young Albert Einstein, Don Brown
Guji Guji, Chih-Yuan Chen
The Neighborhood Mother Goose, Nina Crews
Hot Day on Abbott Avenue, Karen English
The Turn-Around, Upside-Down Alphabet Book, Lisa Campbell Ernst
Sidewalk Circus, Paul Fleischman
Where Is the Green Sheep?, Mem Fox
Kitten's First Full Moon, Kevin Henkes
Apples to Oregon, Deborah Hopkinson
Love and Roast Chicken, Barbara Knutson
The Red Book, Barbara Lehman
Ruby Lu, Brave and True, Lenore Look
Wow! City!, Robert Neubecker
If Not for the Cat, Jack Prelutsky
Tiger on a Tree, Anushka Ravishankar
Lemons Are Not Red, Laura Vaccaro Seeger
Wild About Books, Judy Sierra
Polar Bear Night, Lauren Thompson
Knuffle Bunny: A Cautionary Tale, Mo Willems
Teeth, Tails, & Tentacles, Christopher Wormell

Middle Readers

My Light, Molly Bang
César: ¡Sí, Se Puede! = Yes, We Can!, Carmen T. Bernier-Grand
The Crow-Girl, Bodil Bredsdorff
The Big House, Carolyn Coman
Millions, Frank Cottrell Boyce
Doodler Doodling, Rita Golden Gelman
Technically, It's Not My Fault: Concrete Poems, John Grandits
What Is Goodbye?, Nikki Grimes
The Cats in Krasinski Square, Karen Hesse
Merlin and the Making of the King, Margaret Hodges
The Star of Kazan, Eva Ibbotson
Mable Riley: A Reliable Record of Humdrum, Peril, and Romance,
    Marthe Jocelyn
Walt Whitman: Words for America, Barbara Kerley
Sélavi, That Is Life: A Haitian Story of Hope, Youme Landowne
Fish, L.S. Matthews
The Tarantula Scientist, Sy Montgomery
Remember: The Journey to School Integration, Toni Morrison
Mighty Jackie: The Strike-Out Queen, Marissa Moss
The Little Gentleman, Philippa Pearce
The Boy, the Bear, the Baron, the Bard, Gregory Rogers

Sequoyah: The Cherokee Man Who Gave His People Writing, James Rumford

George vs. George: The American Revolution as Seen from Both Sides, Rosalyn Schanzer

Science Verse, Jon Scieszka

Ellington Was Not a Street, Ntozake Shange

The Train of States, Peter Sis

Coming on Home Soon, Jacqueline Woodson

Older Readers

The Fire-Eaters, David Almond

With Courage and Cloth: Winning the Fight for a Woman's Right to Vote, Ann Bausum

Al Capone Does My Shirts, Gennifer Choldenko

Daniel Half Human and the Good Nazi, David Chotjewitz

Bucking the Sarge, Christopher Paul Curtis

Boy O'Boy, Brian Doyle

Remember D-Day: The Plan, the Invasion, Survivor Stories, Ronald J. Drez

The Sea of Trolls, Nancy Farmer

The Oracle Betrayed, Catherine Fisher

The Voice That Challenged a Nation: Marian Anderson and the Struggle for Equal Rights, Russell Freedman

The Race to Save the Lord God Bird, Phillip M. Hoose

Is This Forever, or What? Poems & Paintings from Texas, ed. Naomi Shihab Nye

Bird, Angela Johnson

Kira-Kira, Cynthia Kadohata

The Outcasts of 19 Schuyler Place, E.L. Konigsburg

Heck Superhero, Martine Leavitt

Indigo's Star, Hilary McKay

A Dream of Freedom: The Civil Rights Movement from 1954 to 1968, Diane McWhorter

Here in Harlem: Poems in Many Voices, Walter Dean Myers

Fortune's Bones: The Manumission Requiem, Marilyn Nelson

Airborn, Kenneth Oppel

The Teacher's Funeral: A Comedy in Three Parts, Richard Peck

A Hat Full of Sky, Terry Pratchett

Becoming Naomi León, Pam Muñoz Ryan

Lizzie Bright and the Buckminster Boy, Gary D. Schmidt

The Schwa Was Here, Neal Shusterman

The Shadows of Ghadames, Joëlle Stolz

So B. It, Sarah Weeks

All Ages

A Child's Christmas in Wales, Dylan Thomas, illustrated by Chris Raschka

Under the Spell of the Moon: Art for Children from the World's Great Illustrators, ed. Patricia Aldana

LANGUAGE

Words About Words

allegory: extended use of symbols, in the form of characters, animals, or events, that represent ideas or themes. Ex: John Bunyan, *Pilgrim's Progress*

alliteration: repetition of same, initial consonant sounds of two or more words in sequence or in short intervals. Ex: "I have *st*ood *st*ill and *st*opped the *s*ound of feet." — Robert Frost

anagram: a word or phrase made by rearranging letters from another word or phrase. Ex: Clint Eastwood = Old West Action.

antithesis: an expression in which contrasting ideas are intentionally juxtaposed, usually in parallel structure. Ex: "The world will little note, nor long remember, what we say here, but it can never forget what they did here." — Abraham Lincoln, "Gettysburg Address"

assonance: repetition of same or similar vowel sounds in words located near each other. Ex: "Gr*ee*n as a dr*ea*m, and d*ee*p as d*ea*th." — Rupert Brooke

cliché: a saying or expression that has been used so often it has lost its effect. Ex: work like a dog

eponym: a word derived from the name of a person. Ex: sandwich, from the Earl of Sandwich.

euphemism: a mild, indirect expression used instead of a plainer one that might be harsh or offensive. Ex: restroom, pass away.

hyperbole: exaggeration for emphasis or effect. Ex: "And fired the shot heard round the world." — Ralph Waldo Emerson, "Concord Hymn"

irony: an expression in which the intended meaning is contrary to its literal meaning; the words say one thing but mean another. Ex: "Yet Brutus says he was ambitious;/ And Brutus is an honorable man." — Shakespeare, *Julius Caesar*

litotes: intentional understatement made by negating the opposite of what is meant. Ex: This was no small matter.

metaphor: implied comparison of two dissimilar things, without using "as" or "like." Ex: "Dawn's rosy fingers" — Homer

metonymy: substitution of one word for another which it suggests. Ex: The pen is mightier than the sword.

onomatopoeia: words that imitate the sounds they describe. Ex: buzz, murmur.

oxymoron: juxtaposition of contradictory words. Ex: deafening silence.

palindrome: a type of anagram in which a word, phrase, or sentence reads the same backward and forward. Ex: Ma is a nun as I am.

paradox: a statement that is seemingly contradictory, odd, or opposed to common sense or expectation and yet is presented as true. Ex: "What a pity that youth must be wasted on the young." — George Bernard Shaw

personification: treating ideas or objects as though they were persons. Ex: "Because I could not stop for Death—/He kindly stopped for me." — Emily Dickinson

portmanteau: two words combined to form one word. Ex: smog (smoke + fog).

simile: a comparison between two dissimilar things using "like" or "as." Ex: "My love is like a red, red rose" — Robert Burns

synecdoche: (a form of metonymy) the use of a part for the whole, or the whole for the part. Ex: All hands on deck!

tautology: unnecessary repetition of an idea in different words, phrases, or sentences. Ex: close proximity.

Foreign Words and Phrases

(F=French; Ger=German; Gk=Greek; I=Italian; L=Latin; S=Spanish; Y=Yiddish)

ad absurdum (L; ad ahb-SUR-dum): to the point of absurdity

ad hoc (L; ad HOK): for the end or purpose at hand; impromptu.

ad hominem (L; ad HOH-mee-nem): emotional rather than intellectual; in a dispute, using slander to obscure issues.

adios (S; ah-di-OHS): goodbye

antebellum (L; AHN-teh-BEL-lum): pre-war

apercu(s) (F; ah-per-SOO): first perception or insight; outline

auf Wiedersehen (Ger; owf-VEE-duh-zehn): Good-bye

belles lettres (F; bel-LET-truh): writing valued for artistic merit

bête noire (F; BET NWAHR): a thing or person viewed with particular dislike or fear

Bildungsroman (Ger; BIL-doongs-roh-mahn): novel with coming-of-age story

bourgeois (F; boo-ZHWAH): middle-class; conventional; materialistic

carte blanche (F; kahrt BLANSH): full discretionary power

cause célèbre (F; kawz suh-LEB-ruh): a notorious incident

cognoscenti (I; koh-nyoh-SHEN-tee): experts; connoissuers

contretemps (F; kon-truh-tahm): awkward situation

coup de grâce (F; kooh duh GRAHS): the final blow

cum laude/magna cum laude/summa cum laude (L; kuhm LOUD-ay; MAGN-a ...; SOO-ma ...): with praise or honor/with great praise or honor/with the highest praise or honor

de facto (L; day FAK-toh): in fact, if not by law

de jure (L; dee JOOR-ee, day YOOR-ay): in accordance with right or law; officially

deo gratias (L; DAY-oh GRAH-tsee-ahs): thanks be to God

de rigueur (F; duh ree-GUR): necessary according to convention or etiquette

détente (F; day-TAHNT): an easing of strained relations

deus ex machina (L; DAY-us eks MAH-keh-nah): a person/event that provides a solution unexpectedly or suddenly, espec. (in literature) a contrived solution to a plot

double entendre (F; DOO-blahn-TAHN-druh): expression with with double meaning, one meaning of which is often risqué

éminence grise (F; ay-meh-nahns-GREEZ): one who wields power behind the scenes

enfant terrible (F; ahn-FAHN te-REE-bluh): one who is noteworthy for embarrassing or unconventional behavior

ennui (F; ah-NOOEE); boredom; world-weariness; annoyance

e pluribus unum (L; eh-PLOO-ree-boos-OO-noom): out of many, one (U.S. motto)

ersatz (Ger; EHR-zats): artificial, inferior

esprit de corps (F; es-PREE duh KAWR): group spirit; feeling of camaraderie

eureka (Gk; yoor-EE-kuh): I have found it!; hurrah!

ex post facto (L; eks pohst FAK-toh): retroactive(ly)

fait accompli (F; fayt uh-kom-PLEE): an accomplished fact

faux pas (F; foh PAH): as false step; a social blunder or breach of etiquette

habeas corpus (L; HAY-bee-ahs KOR-pus): an order for an accused person to be brought to court

hasta la vista (S; asta-la-VIS-ta): goodbye

hoi polloi (Gk; hoy puh-LOY): the masses

in loco parentis (L; in LOH-koh puh-REN-tis): in place of parent

in omnibus (L; in OHM-nee-bus): in all things; in all ways

je ne sais quoi (F; zhuh nuh say KWAH): I don't know what; the little something that eludes description

joie de vivre (F; zhwah duh VEEV-ruh): zest for life

mano a mano (S; MAH-noh ah MAH-noh): hand to hand; in direct combat

mea culpa (L; MAY-uh CUL-puh): through my fault

mensch (Y; mentsh): an upright, noble, admirable person

modus operandi (L; MOH-duhs op-uh-RAN-dee): method of operation

noblesse oblige (F; noh-BLES oh-BLEEZH): the obligation of nobility to help the less fortunate

nolo contendere (L; NOH-loh-kohn-TEN-deh-reh): "I will not contest," a plea of no defense, equivalent to a plea of guilty.

non compos mentis (L; non KOM-puhs MEN-tis): not of sound mind

non sequitur (L; non SEH-kwi-tour): a conclusion that does not logically follow from what preceded it

nouveau riche (F; noo-voh REESH): a person newly rich, perhaps one who spends money conspicuously

par excellence (F; par ek-seh-LANS): best of all; incomparable.

parvenu (F; par-vuh-NOO): upstart

persona non grata (L; per-SOH-nah non GRAH-tah): unwelcome person

pièce de résistance (F; pee-es duh ray-ZEES-tonz): the outstanding item in a series or group

pro bono (L; proh BOH-noh): (legal work) donated for the public good

qué será será (S; keh sair-AH sair-AH): what will be will be

quid pro quo (L; kwid proh KWOH): something given or received for something else

raison d'être (F; RAY-zohnn DET-ruh): reason for being

sans souci (F; SAHNN sooh-SEE): without worry

savoir faire (F; sav-wahr-FAIR): dexterity in social affairs

Schadenfreude (Ger; SHAH-d'n-froy-deh): joy at another's misfortune

schlemiel (Y; shleh-MEEL): an unlucky, bungling person

schlepp (Y; shlep): move slowly, tediously, drag oneself along

semper fidelis (L; SEM-puhr fee-DAY-lis): always faithful

sobriquet (F; soh-bree-KAY): nickname

terra firma (L; TER-uh FUR-muh): solid ground

tour de force (F; TOOR duh FAWRS): feat accomplished through great skill

vis-à-vis (F; vee-zuh-VEE): compared with; with regard to

zeitgeist (Ger; ZITE-gyste): the general intellectual, moral, and cultural climate of an era

Commonly Misspelled English Words

accidentally	Cincinnati	existence
accommodate	collectible	fascinating
acknowledgment	commitment	feasible
acquainted	committee	February
acquire	connoisseur	fluorine
across	conscientious	foreign
all right	conscious	forty
already	convenience	gauge
amateur	deceive	government
appearance	defendant	grammar
appropriate	definitely	grateful
bureau	desirable	harass
business	despair	humorous
calendar	desperate	hurrying
Caribbean	eligible	incidentally
cemetery	eliminate	independent
changeable	embarrass	indispensable
chrysanthemum	environment	inoculate

irresistible
judgment
laboratory
leisure
library
license
lieutenant
lightning
liquefy
maintenance
marriage
medieval
millennium
miniature
miscellaneous
Mississippi
misspelled
mnemonic

mysterious
necessary
noticeable
occasionally
occurrence
opportunity
optimistic
parallel
performance
permanent
permissible
perseverance
personnel
possess
privilege
propaganda
questionnaire
receipt

receive
restaurant
rhythm
ridiculous
separate
seize
sincerely
stubbornness
supersede
tangible
temperament
temperature
transferred
truly
twelfth
Wednesday
weird
wholly

Commonly Confused English Words

adverse: unfavorable
averse: opposed

affect: to influence
effect: to bring about

allusion: an indirect reference
illusion: an unreal impression

appraise: to set a value on
apprise: to inform

biannual: occurring twice a year
biennial: occurring every two years

capital: the seat of government
capitol: building where a legislature meets

complement: to make complete; something that completes
compliment: to praise; praise

counselor: one who gives advice or counsel
councilor: a member of a council

denote: to mean
connote: to suggest beyond the explicit meaning

discreet: prudent
discrete: separate, distinct

disinterested: impartial
uninterested: without interest

elicit: to draw or bring out
illicit: illegal

emigrate: to leave for another place
immigrate: to come to another place

ensure: to make certain
insure: to protect against
assure: to inform postively or confidently

exalt: to glorify
exult: to rejoice

farther: at a greater distance
further: to a greater extent or degree

fewer: a smaller *number* (of things)
less: a smaller *amount* (of something)

grisly: inspiring horror or great fear
grizzly: sprinkled or streaked with gray

historic: important in history
historical: relating to history

hoard: a supply stored up and often hidden
horde: a teeming croud or throng

I: nominative case
me: objective case

immanent: inherent; residing within
imminent: ready to take place
eminent: standing out

imply: to suggest but not explicitly
infer: to assume or understand information not relayed explicitly

include: used when the items following are part of a whole
comprise: used when the items following are all of a whole

ingenious: clever
ingenuous: innocent

it's: it is
its: a possessive adjective

lay: to put or place
lie: (intransitive) to recline or rest

oral: spoken, as opposed to written
verbal: relating to language

principal: n., business owner, head of school; adj., most important
principle: a basic law or truth; a moral or ethical standard

their: belonging to them
there: in that place
they're: they are

who: nominative case
whom: objective case

your: belonging to you
you're: you are

HISTORY

History of Books & Printing

Source: *Funk & Wagnalls New Encyclopedia*

BOOK, a volume of many sheets bound together, containing text, illustration, or music. Unlike an inscribed monument, a book is portable; and unlike a private diary, which may be in book form, it is intended for circulation. A book is larger than a pamphlet and is a single independent unit as distinguished from a periodical.

Handwritten Books

The forerunners of books were the clay tablets, impressed with a stylus, used by the Sumerians, Babylonians, and other peoples of ancient Mesopotamia. Much more closely related to the modern book were the book rolls, or scrolls, of the ancient Egyptians, Greeks, and Romans, which consisted of sheets of papyrus, a paperlike material made from the pounded pith of reeds growing in the Nile River delta.

Although papyrus was easily made, inexpensive, and an excellent writing surface, it was brittle. Parchment and vellum (especially prepared animal skins) did not have those drawbacks. The Persians, Hebrews, and other peoples of the ancient Middle East, where papyrus did not grow, had for centuries used scrolls made of tanned leather or untanned parchment. By the 4th century ad, parchment had almost entirely supplanted papyrus as a medium for writing.

The Early Codex

The 4th century also marked the culmination of a gradual process, begun about the 1st century, in which the inconvenient scroll was replaced by the rectangular codex (Lat., "book"), the direct ancestor of the modern book. The codex, as first used by the Greeks and Romans for business accounts or school work, was a small, ringed notebook consisting of two or more wooden tablets covered with wax, which could be marked with a stylus, smoothed over, and reused many times.

Medieval European Books

In the early Middle Ages in Europe books were written chiefly by churchmen for other churchmen and for rulers. Many medieval books were brilliantly illuminated in gold and colors to indicate the start of a new section of text, to illustrate the text, or to decorate the borders, such as the all-over, intricately stylized ornament of the Book of Kells (Trinity College, Dublin), an 8th- to 9th-century copy of the Gospels made in Scotland and Ireland.

Books in the Orient

Perhaps the earliest form of book in the Far East was wood or bamboo tablets tied with cord. Another early form was strips of silk or paper, a mixture of bark and hemp invented by the Chinese in the 2d century AD. At first the strips, written on one side only with a reed pen or brush, were wound around sticks to make scrolls. Later they were also folded like an accordion and stitched on one side to make a book, which was glued to a light paper- or cloth-covered case.

Printed Books

Printing from carved wood blocks was invented in China in the 6th century AD. In the 11th century the Chinese also invented printing from movable type, which, unlike the early wood blocks that could be used for only one work, could be reassembled in different orders for numerous works. In Europe the printing of books from wood blocks, a technique probably learned from contact with the East, began in the late Middle Ages.

Renaissance Books

In the 15th century the development of paper and movable metal type revolutionized the production of European books. The Europeans learned about paper from the Muslim world (which had acquired it from China). Movable metal type was invented independently by the Europeans. Although various claims have been put forth for French, Italian, and Dutch inventors, the German printer Johann Gutenberg is usually given the credit, and the first major book printed in movable type was the Gutenberg Bible (1456). These innovations made book production economically feasible and relatively easy, and public literacy increased greatly.

Italian Renaissance printers of the 16th century set traditions that have persisted in book publishing since that time, such as the use of light pasteboard covers, often bound in leather, of regularized layouts, and of clear Roman and Italic typefaces. Woodcuts and engravings were used for illustrations. Renaissance books also established the convention of the title page and the preface, or introduction.

Contemporary Books

Since the Industrial Revolution, book production has become highly mechanized. The more efficient manufacture of paper, the introduction of cloth and paper covers, high-speed cylinder presses, the mechanical casting and composing of type, phototypesetting, and photographic reproduction of both text and illustration have made possible the production in the 20th century of vast numbers of books at a relatively low price

Books as a means of communication were challenged by such 20th-century inventions as radio, television, films, and tape recorders. In addition, from the time it first became available to consumers in the mid-1990s, the Internet became an increasingly valuable source of information. There were predictions that sales of electronic books, or e-books, could pose a particular challenge, and weblogs, or blogs, became increasingly popular as mediums of expression. Nonetheless, traditional books remained the primary vehicle for dissemination of knowledge and for the recording of experience, whether real or imagined. Books continued to sell, and in some cases their sales were fueled by opportunities to purchase them, and read about them, on the Internet.

MOST INFLUENTIAL BOOKS

World Almanac editors selected the following books as those that had the greatest influence on history

1. *The Bible*

2. *The Koran*

3. *On the Origin of Species by Means of Natural Selection, or The Preservation of Favoured Races in the Struggle for Life* (1859), Charles Darwin

4. *The Communist Manifesto* (1848), Karl Marx & Friedrich Engels

5. *The Republic* (360 B.C.), Plato

6. *Mein Kampf* (1925), Adolf Hitler

7. *The 95 Theses (Disputation of Doctor Martin Luther on the Power and Efficacy of Indulgences)* (1517), Martin Luther

8. *Two Treatises of Government* (1680-1690), John Locke

9. *Relativity: The Special and General Theory* (1905 & 1915), Albert Einstein

10. *The Prince* (1532), Niccolo Machiavelli

The Ten Greatest Works of Literature of the Second Millennium

By John Updike

Source: *The World Almanac and Book of Facts 2000*

John Updike, the acclaimed American novelist, short-story writer, poet, and literary critic, is perhaps best known for his "Rabbit" novels, beginning with *Rabbit, Run* (1960), and ending with *Rabbit at Rest* (1990), one of two novels for which he won a Pulitzer Prize. His literary criticism is displayed in such works as *More Matter* (1999).

Selections are listed chronologically.

Thomas Aquinas, *Summa Theologica*, written c. 1265-73.

Dante Alighieri, *The Divine Comedy*, written c. 1307-21.

Miguel de Cervantes Saavedra, *Don Quixote, Part I*, 1605; Part II, 1615.

William Shakespeare, *Comedies, Histories, and Tragedies*, written c. 1590-1613, published 1623.

Voltaire, *Candide*, 1759.

Edward Gibbon, *The History of the Decline and Fall of the Roman Empire,* 1776-88.

Leo Tolstoy, *War and Peace*, 1865-69.

Fyodor Dostoyevsky, *The Possessed*, 1871-72.

Marcel Proust, *Remembrance of Things Past*, 1913-27.

James Joyce, *Ulysses*, 1922.

History of The World Almanac

THE WORLD ALMANAC AND BOOK OF FACTS is an American institution that tens of millions of people have turned to since 1868. Here is a brief history of **THE WORLD ALMANAC**, along with a few interesting facts:

• The first edition of *The World Almanac* was published by *The New York World* newspaper in 1868. The name of the publication comes from the newspaper itself. Published just three years after the end of the Civil War and the assassination of President Abraham Lincoln, the first WORLD ALMANAC offered 120 pages of information, covering such events as the process of Reconstruction and the impeachment of President Andrew Johnson.

• Publication was suspended in 1876, but in 1886 famed newspaper publisher **Joseph Pulitzer**, who had purchased *The New York World* and quickly transformed it into one of the most influential newspapers in the country, revived *The World Almanac* with the intention of making it "a compendium of universal knowledge." *The World Almanac* has been published annually ever since.

• In 1923 after Warren Harding's sudden death, **Calvin Coolidge** was sworn in as president by his father, a Vermont notary public, who read the oath of office from a copy of *The World Almanac*.

• During World War II, *The World Almanac* could boast that it was read by GIs all over the world: between 1944 and 1946, at the request of the U.S. Government, *The World Almanac* had special print runs of 100,000 to 150,000 copies for **distribution to the armed forces**.

• In 1961, a wire service photograph showed **President Kennedy** sitting behind his desk in the Oval Office and on his desk were 6 books: the only reference book was *The World Almanac*. Amazingly, almost 40 years later, a 1999 New York Times photo showed **President Clinton** in almost the exact same position, seated at his desk in the Oval Office. Clearly visible on the desk behind him are busts of Jefferson and Lincoln, pictures of his wife and daughter, a Bible, and a copy of *The World Almanac*. And they're not the only U.S. Presidents who have relied on *The World Almanac*: at **Franklin Roosevelt's** home in Hyde Park, NY, a reproduction of his White House desk includes a copy of *The World Almanac* 1945.

• Over the years *The World Almanac* has become a household name and has been featured in a number of Hollywood films. For example, Fred MacMurray talks about it with Edward G. Robinson in *Double Indemnity*; Bette Davis screams about it in *All About Eve*; Audrey Hepburn and Gary Cooper flirt about it in *Love in the Afternoon*; it is featured in *Miracle on 34th Street* when a trial is held to see if Santa Claus really exists; and Rosie Perez continually reads it in the film *White Men Can't Jump*. *The World Almanac* also makes frequent appearances on television. It was recently featured on *Wheel of Fortune* as a puzzle title. It is regularly cited as a source on *Jeopardy!* and also provides a key source for contestants preparing for that show.

• Today, *The World Almanac* continues to top best-seller lists and remains the top-selling American reference book of all time.

LIBRARIES

100 Largest Libraries in U.S. by Volumes Held, 2003

Source: American Library Association, *ALA Library Fact Sheet 22*, August 2005.

Ranked at end of the 2003 fiscal year.

	Institution	Volumes Held*
1.	Library of Congress	29,550,914
2.	Harvard University	15,181,349
3.	Boston Public Library	14,933,349
4.	Yale University	11,114,308
5.	Chicago Public Library	10,745,608
6.	University of Illinois - Urbana-Champaign	10,015,321
7.	Public Library of Cincinnati & Hamilton County	9,885,359
8.	Queens Borough Public Library	9,691,126
9.	University of California - Berkeley	9,572,462
10.	County of Los Angeles Public Library	9,185,321
11.	University of Texas - Austin	8,322,944
12.	Stanford University	8,000,000
13.	University of Michigan	7,800,389
14.	Columbia University	7,697,488
15.	University of California - Los Angeles	7,576,790
16.	Detroit Public Library	7,265,306
17.	University of Wisconsin - Madison	7,232,850
18.	Cornell University	7,120,301
19.	University of Chicago	6,977,186
20.	New York Public Library	6,777,587
21.	Indiana University	6,647,355
22.	University of Washington	6,436,960
23.	Free Library of Philadelphia	6,388,077
24.	Princeton University	6,224,270
25.	University of Minnesota	6,200,669
26.	Dallas Public Library	5,916,549
27.	Brooklyn Public Library	5,845,212
28.	Ohio State University	5,674,784
29.	Los Angeles Public Library	5,554,904
30.	University of North Carolina - Chapel Hill	5,492,451
31.	Duke University	5,360,303
32.	University of Pennsylvania	5,273,887
33.	University of Arizona	5,040,584
34.	University of Virginia	4,921,442
35.	Pennsylvania State University Libraries	4,779,165
36.	Michigan State University	4,582,004
37.	University of Oklahoma	4,427,670
38.	University of Pittsburgh	4,420,970
39.	University of Iowa	4,380,734
40.	Houston Public Library	4,339,128
41.	Northwestern University Library	4,315,314
42.	King County Library System	4,213,810
43.	New York University	4,176,065
44.	Rutgers University	4,050,009
45.	University of Florida	4,021,629
46.	Cleveland Public Library	3,999,771
47.	Miami-Dade Public Library System	3,998,192
48.	University of Kansas	3,980,589
49.	University of Georgia	3,955,004

Institution	Volumes Held*
50. Arizona State University Libraries	3,856,561
51. University of Southern California	3,800,702
52. Washington University - St. Louis	3,608,538
53. Johns Hopkins University	3,572,375
54. Buffalo & Erie County Public Library	3,539,038
55. Cuyahoga County Public Library	3,465,469
56. University of South Carolina	3,374,496
57. Brigham Young University	3,373,793
58. University of California - Davis	3,365,689
59. St. Louis Public Library	3,360,942
60. State University of New York - Buffalo	3,330,476
61. Wayne State University	3,323,580
62. University of Colorado	3,314,432
63. University of Hawaii	3,294,184
64. Hawaii State Public Library System	3,281,117
65. Brown University	3,257,242
66. North Carolina State University	3,236,096
67. Louisiana State University	3,213,314
68. University of Rochester	3,185,231
69. San Diego Public Library	3,169,565
70. University of Connecticut	3,168,617
71. University of Missouri - Columbia	3,149,211
72. University of Massachusetts	3,132,418
73. University of Utah	3,128,547
74. Mid-Continent Public Library	3,120,544
75. University of Notre Dame	3,054,075
76. University of Kentucky	3,053,726
77. University of Maryland	3,016,940
78. Texas A&M University Libraries	3,016,358
79. Milwaukee Public Library	2,989,081
80. University of Cincinnati Libraries	2,977,475
81. Montgomery County Dept. of Public Libraries	2,959,184
82. Columbus Metropolitan Library	2,955,569
83. University of California - San Diego	2,953,024
84. Enoch Pratt Free Library	2,906,821
85. Temple University	2,900,832
86. Syracuse University	2,900,448
87. Vanderbilt University	2,882,057
88. University of Tennessee - Knoxville	2,880,949
89. Broward County Libraries Division	2,825,077
90. Orange County Public Library	2,794,942
91. Southern Illinois University - Carbondale	2,791,775
92. St. Louis County Library District	2,781,301
93. University of Nebraska - Lincoln	2,767,320
94. University of California - Santa Barbara	2,765,756
95. Emory University	2,755,929
96. Auburn University	2,724,011
97. Fairfax County Public Library	2,712,212
98. Massachusetts Institute of Technology	2,707,849
99. Toledo-Lucas County Public Library	2,689,922
100. Kent State University Libraries	2,634,374

*Figures for public libraries include holdings by branches and include circulating books only.

Dewey Decimal Classification®

In library science, a method of classifying knowledge for the purpose of cataloging books and other library materials, devised by Melvil Dewey. Under this system all knowledge is divided into ten main classes, each of which is designated by a 100-number span. Each main class is divided into ten subclasses.

Example: *The World Almanac and Book of Facts for Booklovers* would be classified as 002.03

Top 10 Classes of the Dewey Decimal Classification

Class	Caption
000	Computer science, information & general works
100	Philosophy & psychology
200	Religion
300	Social sciences
400	Language
500	Science
600	Technology
700	Arts & recreation
800	Literature
900	History & geography

All copyright rights in The Dewey Decimal Classification are owned by OCLC Online Computer Library Center, Inc. Used with permission. DDC, Dewey and Dewey Decimal Classification are registered trademarks of OCLC Online Computer Library Center, Inc.

Library of Congress Classification

In the Library of Congress Classification system (familiarly known as LC), all knowledge is divided into 21 large classes, indicated more or less arbitrarily by capital letters. Within each of these classes, material is arranged from general considerations to specific treatments and from theory to practical applications; specific topics are indicated by means of combinations of capital letters, and further subject breakdowns by 3-digit numbers. The classification scheme is continuously revised.

Example: How can you determine what book QE 534.2 B64 is? The Q indicates Science and the QE indicates Geology. By looking at the first numbers, 534.2, we know this falls under the geology subcategory "Dynamic and Structural Geology: Earthquakes and Volcanoes." The next number is called the Cutter Number and it is a coded representation of the author or organization's name or the title of the work. The Cutter Number of "B64" represents the book *Earthquakes* by Bruce A. Bolt.

A:	General Works	N:	Fine Arts
B:	Philosophy; Religion	P:	Language and Literature
C:	History: Auxiliary Sciences	Q:	Science
D:	Universal History	R:	Medicine
E,F:	American History	S:	Agriculture
G:	Geography; Anthropology	T:	Technology
H:	Social Sciences	U:	Military Science
J:	Political Sciences	V:	Naval Science
K:	Law	Z:	Bibliography and Library
L:	Education		Science
M:	Music		

Presidential Libraries

The libraries listed here, except for that of Richard Nixon (which is private), are coordinated by the National Archives and Records Administration (Website: www.archives.gov/presidential_libraries/index.html). NARA also has custody of the Nixon presidential historical materials and those of Bill Clinton. The William J. Clinton Library opened in Nov. 2004. NARA will release Clinton presidential records to the public at the Clinton Library beginning Jan. 20, 2006. Materials for presidents before Herbert Hoover are held by private institutions.

Herbert Hoover Library and Museum
210 Parkside Dr., West Branch, IA 52358, Phone: 319-643-5301
E-mail: hoover.library@nara.gov, Website: www.hoover.archives.gov

Franklin D. Roosevelt Library and Museum
4079 Albany Post Rd,; Hyde Park, NY 12538-1990; 845-486-7770, 1-800-FDR-VISIT
E-mail: roosevelt.library@nara.gov, Website: www.fdrlibrary.marist.edu

Harry S. Truman Library and Museum
500 West U.S. Hwy. 24; Independence, MO 64050-2481; 816-268-8200, 1-800-833-1225
E-mail: truman.library@nara.gov, Website: www.trumanlibrary.org

Dwight D. Eisenhower Library
200 S.E. 4th St., Abilene, KS 67410-2900; 785-263-6700; 1-877-RING-IKE
E-mail: eisenhower.library@nara.gov, Website:
www.eisenhower.archives.gov

John Fitzgerald Kennedy Library
Columbia Pt., Boston, MA 02125-3398; 617-514-1600; 1-866-JFK-1960
E-mail: kennedy.library@nara.gov, Website: www.jfklibrary.org

Lyndon Baines Johnson Library and Museum
2313 Red River St., Austin, TX 78705-5702; 512-721-0200
E-mail: johnson.library@nara.gov, Website: www.lbjlib.utexas.edu

Richard Nixon Library & Birthplace
18001 Yorba Linda Blvd., Yorba Linda, CA 92886; 714-993-5075
E-mail: archives@nixonlibrary.org, Website: www.nixonfoundation.org

Gerald R. Ford Library
1000 Beal Ave., Ann Arbor, MI 48109-2114; 734-205-0555
E-mail: ford.library@nara.gov, Website: www.fordlibrarymuseum.gov

Jimmy Carter Library
441 Freedom Pkwy., Atlanta, GA 30307-1498; 404-865-7100
E-mail: carter.library@nara.gov, Website: www.jimmycarterlibrary.org

Ronald Reagan Library
40 Presidential Dr., Simi Valley, CA 93065-0600; 800-410-8354
E-mail: reagan.library@nara.gov, Website: www.reagan.utexas.edu

George H. W. Bush Library
1000 George Bush Dr. West, College Station, TX 77845; 979-691-4000
E-mail: bush.library@nara.gov, Website: bush.library.tamu.edu

William J. Clinton Library and Museum
1200 President Clinton Ave., Little Rock, AR 72201; 501-374-4242
E-mail: clinton.library@nara.gov,Website: www.clintonlibrary.gov

MAGAZINES & LITERARY JOURNALS

Bestselling U.S. Magazines, 2004

Source: Audit Bureau of Circulations, Schaumburg, IL

General magazines, exclusive of comics; also excluding magazines that failed to file reports to ABC by press time. Based on total average paid circulation during the 6 months ending Dec. 31, 2004.

	Publication	Paid circ.
1.	AARP The Magazine	22,617,093
2.	AARP Bulletin	22,181,859
3.	Reader's Digest	10,081,577
4.	TV Guide	9,015,544
5.	Better Homes and Gardens	7,626,088
6.	National Geographic	5,475,135
7.	Good Housekeeping	4,639,941
8.	Woman's Day	4,209,130
9.	Family Circle	4,147,657
10.	Ladies' Home Journal	4,120,087
11.	Time	4,034,061
12.	People	3,652,022
13.	Sports Illustrated	3,324,631
14.	Home & Away	3,317,597
15.	Prevention	3,309,110
16.	Newsweek	3,125,971
17.	Playboy	3,051,344
18.	Cosmopolitan	2,982,508
19.	Southern Living	2,730,437
20.	Guideposts	2,659,733
21.	O, The Oprah Magazine	2,650,464
22.	Maxim	2,517,126
23.	Redbook	2,407,985
24.	Glamour	2,397,508
25.	Seventeen	2,108,292
26.	Game Informer	2,045,912
27.	Smithsonian	2,044,856
28.	Parenting	2,028,950
29.	U.S. News & World Report	2,014,422
30.	Parents	1,989,512
31.	Money	1,924,414
32.	Martha Stewart Living	1,894,134
33.	Real Simple	1,809,792
34.	ESPN The Magazine	1,792,359
35.	Entertainment Weekly	1,791,163
36.	Familyfun	1,739,121
37.	Country Living	1,728,962
38.	In Style	1,728,522
39.	Endless Vacation	1,695,852
40.	Cooking Light	1,680,573
41.	Men's Health	1,666,245

	Publication	Paid circ.
42.	Ebony	1,630,248
43.	YM	1,627,764
44.	Woman's World	1,622,084
45.	Shape	1,618,516
46.	Golf Digest	1,577,757
47.	Teen People	1,560,480
48.	Field & Stream	1,524,897
49.	First For Women	1,513,414
50.	Fitness	1,488,849

American Literary Journals

Oldest American Literary Journal

North American Review

Literary Slicks

The Atlantic
Esquire
GQ

Harper's
The New Yorker
Playboy

Most Prominent Literary Journals

Bomb
Agni
Conjunctions
Granta

One Story
The Paris Review
The Threepenny Review
Zoetrope

Quietly Influential Literary Journals

American Letters & Commentary
The Antioch Review
Black Warrior Review
Boulevard
Chicago Review
Creative Nonfiction
Georgia Review
Gettysburg Review
Hudson Review
Indiana Review
The Iowa Review

Kenyon Review
Michigan Quarterly Review
The Missouri Review
New England Review
Ploughshares
Quarterly West
Raritan
The Southern Review
TriQuarterly
Witness
The Yale Review

Up and Coming

A Public Space
Black Clock
The Cincinnati Review

The Common Review
Quick Fiction

Quirkiest Journals

The Believer
Fence
McSweeney's

Paragraph
The Sun
Tin House

INTERNET DIRECTORY TO SELECTED SITES

The websites listed are but a sampling of what is available. You may also find suggested websites of interest in the free monthly World Almanac E-Newsletter, available at www.worldalmanac.com.

You must type an address exactly as written. You may be unable to connect to a site because (1) you have mistyped the address, (2) the site is busy, or (3) it has moved or no longer exists. (Addresses are subject to change, and sites or products are not endorsed by *The World Almanac*.)

Audio Books
AudioBooksForFree   www.audiobooksforfree.com

Author Websites
Isabel Allende   www.isabelallende.com
Maya Angelou   www.mayaangelou.com
Ray Bradbury   www.raybradbury.com
Barbara Taylor Bradford   www.barbarataylorbradford.com
Dan Brown   www.danbrown.com
A.S. Byatt   www.asbyatt.com
Michael Chabon   www.michaelchabon.com
Michael Connelly   www.michaelconnelly.com
Patricia Cornwell   www.patriciacornwell.com
Gail Godwin   www.gailgodwin.com
Michael Crichton   www.crichton-official.com
Michael Cunningham   www.michaelcunninghamwriter.com
Nelson DeMille   www.nelsondemille.net
Ken Follett   www.ken-follett.com
Jonathan Franzen   www.jonathanfranzen.com
Sue Grafton   www.suegrafton.com
Václav Havel   www.vaclavhavel.cz
Tony Hillerman   www.tonyhillermanbooks.com
John Jakes   www.johnjakes.com
Stephen King   www.stephenking.com
Barbara Kingsolver   www.kingsolver.com
Madeleine L'Engle   www.madeleinelengle.com
Elmore Leonard   www.elmoreleonard.com
Gregory Maguire   www.gregorymaguire.com
Armistead Maupin   www.literarybent.com
Cormac McCarthy   www.cormacmccarthy.com
Ian McEwan   www.ianmcewan.com
Terry McMillan   www.terrymcmillan.com
Walter Mosley   www.waltermosley.com
Marge Piercy   www.margepiercy.com
Annie Proulx   www.annieproulx.com
Anne Rice   www.annerice.com
J.K. Rowling   www.jkrowling.com
Kurt Vonnegut   www.vonnegut.com
Edmund White   www.edmundwhite.com
Tom Wolfe   www.tomwolfe.com

Bestseller Lists
Barnes & Noble Bestsellers www.barnesandnoble.com/bestsellers
Bestseller Lists 1900-1995 www.caderbooks.com/bestintro.html
The New York Times Bestseller Lists www.nytimes.com/pages/books/bestseller/
USA Today Best Selling Books www.usatoday.com/life/books/top-50.htm

Blogs: Literature and the Publishing World

BookBlog   www.bookblog.net
Buzz, Balls & Hype   mjroseblog.typepad.com/buzz_balls_hype
Conversational Reading   esposito.typepad.com/con_read
Cup O'Books   www.cupobooks.com
Fresh Eyes: A Bookseller's Journal   www.publishersmarketplace.com/members/shire15
I'm Not Really A Waitress   www.publishersmarketplace.com/members/Patry
John Kremer on Marketing   www.publishersmarketplace.com/members/JohnKremer
The Literary Saloon   www.complete-review.com/saloon
Maude Newton   www.maudnewton.com/blog
Mind Scrabble   www.publishersmarketplace.com/members/ElizRN
Moby Lives   www.mobylives.com
Rants, Raves and Random Thoughts   www.publishersmarketplace.com/members/jamesgoodman
The Reader's Muse   reader.blogspot.com
Vestige.org   www.vestige.org
Write News   www.writenews.com/blog
Writer's Write   www.writerswrite.com/writersblog

Book Reviews

ALA Booklist   www.ala.org/ala/booklist/booklist.htm
The Beat   www.kuow.org/thebeat_books.asp
Biblioreview.com   www.biblioreview.com
BookBrowse   www.bookbrowse.com
BookBrowser   www.barnesandnoble.com/bookbrowser
BookPage   www.bookpage.com
The Bookreporter   www.bookreporter.com
BookSpot   www.bookspot.com
The Boston Book Review   www.bookwire.com/bookwire/bbr/bbr-home.html
Comics Worth Reading   www.comicsworthreading.com
ForeWord   www.forewordmagazine.com
The Mystery Reader   www.themysteryreader.com
Nabou   bookreviews.nabou.com
The New York Review of Books   www.nybooks.com
The New York Times Book Review   www.nytimes.com/pages/books
PAGESOnline   www.ireadpages.com
QBR: The Black Book Review Online   www.qbr.com
Reviews of Books   www.reviewsofbooks.com
The Romance Reader   www.theromancereader.com

Book Signings

Bookends   www.powerpg.com/bk
Celebrity Book Signings & Events   www.geocities.com/leecoke/
Readerville   www.readerville.com

Bookstores—New and Used

Abebooks.com   www.abebooks.com
AddALL   www.addall.com
Alibris   www.alibris.com
Allbookstores.com   www.allbookstores.com
Amazon.com Inc.   www.amazon.com
Antiquarian Booksellers Association of America   abaa.org
Barnes & Noble   www.barnesandnoble.com
Best Book Buys   www.bestwebbuys.com/books
Biblio   biblio.com

BookFinder.com www.bookfinder.com
BookFinder4U.com www.bookfinder4u.com
Booksamillion www.booksamillion.com
Booksense (Independent Bookstores) www.booksense.com
Borders www.bordersstores.com
FetchBook.info www.fetchbook.info
Half.com www.half.com
HamiltonBook.com www.hamiltonbook.com
Powell's City of Books www.powells.com

Chat Sites

Book Chat www.4-lane.com/bookchat
Salon.com Table Talk tabletalk.salon.com

Children's Author Websites

Avi www.avi-writer.com
Stan & Jan Berenstain www.berenstainbears.com
Jan Brett www.janbrett.com
The Lewis Carroll Page www.lewiscarroll.org/carroll.html
Beverly Cleary www.beverlycleary.com
Roald Dahl www.roalddahl.com
Patricia Polacco www.patriciapolacco.com
Shel Silverstein www.shelsilverstein.com
Lemony Snickett www.lemonysnicket.com
William Steig www.williamsteig.com
Laura Ingalls Wilder www.liwms.com

Children's Sites

Children's Book Awards www.ucalgary.ca/~dkbrown/awards.html
Children's Television Workshop www.sesameworkshop.org
Judy Blume's Home Base www.judyblume.com
International Wizard of Oz Club www.ozclub.org
Just For Kids Who Love Books www.alanbrown.com
The Newbery Medal www.ala.org/alsc/newbery.html
Peace Corps Kids World www.peacecorps.gov/kids
J.K. Rowling www.jkrowling.com
Seussville www.seussville.com
SuperSite for Kids www.bonus.com
Weekly Reader www.weeklyreader.com
White House for Kids www.whitehousekids.gov
World Almanac for Kids www.worldalmanacforkids.com
Yahooligans (for homework help) www.yahooligans.com

Dictionary & Word Sites

Acronym & Abbreviation Server www.ucc.ie/cgi-bin/acronym/
index.html
Acronym Finder www.acronymfinder.com
Cambridge Dictionaries www.yourdictionary.com
Dictionary.com dictionary.reference.com
Encarta (talking) encarta.msn.com/encnet/features/dictionary/
dictionaryhome.aspx
Glossary of Poetic Terms www.poeticbyway.com/glossary.html
Idiom Site www.idiomsite.com
Medi-Lexicon www.medilexicon.com
Merriam-Webster Online www.m-w.com
One Look Dictionary Search www.onelook.com
Roget's Thesaurus thesaurus.reference.com
YourDictionary.com www.yourdictionary.com

Digital Libraries: International Texts

ABU: la Bibliothëque Universelle (French Texts)   abu.cnam.fr
Ceska citanka (Czech Texts)   citanka.cz
Corpus of Electronic Texts (Irish Texts)   www.ucc.ie/celt
National Diet Library (Japan)   www.ndl.go.jp/en/data/endl.html
Project Runeburg (Nordic Literature)   runeberg.org
Russica Miscellanea (Russian)   home.freeuk.com/russica2/index.html
South Slavic Literature Library   www.borut.com/library/
Virtual Library of Polish Literature   monika.univ.gda.pl/~literat/
World's Literature   www.griffe.com/projects/worldlit/

Literary Awards

Academy of American Poets Awards   www.poets.org
Agatha Awards   www.malicedomestic.org/agatha.htm
Astrid Lindgren Memorial Award   www.alma.se/
Asian American Literary Awards   www.aaww.org/litawards/
   recipients.html
AwardWeb   dpsinfo.com/awardweb/
Bram Stoker Award   www.horror.org/stokers.htm
Caldecott Awards   www.ala.org/ala/alsc/awardsscholarships/
   literaryawds/caldecottmedal/caldecottmedal.htm
Edgar Award   www.mysterywriters.org/pages/awards/index.htm
The Golden Kite Awards   www.scbwi.org/awards/gk_main.htm
Harvey Awards   harveyawards.org/
Hugo Award   www.wsfs.org/hugos.html
Lambda Literary Foundation   www.lambdalit.org/index_2.html
Man Booker Awards   www.themanbookerprize.com/
National Book Award   www.nationalbook.org/nba.html
National Book Critics Circle Award   www.bookcritics.org/page2.html
Nebula Awards   www.sfwa.org/awards/
Newbury Awards   www.ala.org/ala/alsc/awardsscholarships/
   literaryawds/newberymedal/newberymedal.htm
Nobel Prizes   nobelprize.org/
PEN/Faulkner Awards   www.penfaulkner.org/
Pulitzer Prize   www.pulitzer.org/
Stonewall Book Awards   www.ala.org/ala/glbtrt/stonewall/
   stonewallbook.htm
Whitbread Book Awards   www.whitbread-bookawards.co.uk/

News

The Associated Press   www.ap.org
BBC Online   news.bbc.co.uk
Cable News Network   www.cnn.com
The Los Angeles Times   www.latimes.com
MSNBC   www.msnbc.com
The New York Times   www.nytimes.com
Reuters   www.reuters.com
USA Today   www.usatoday.com
Washington Post   www.washingtonpost.com
World Press Review Online   www.worldpress.org

Playwrights

Playwrights on the Web   www.stageplays.com/writers.htm
Theatre USA   theatreusa.com/

Reference

About.com   www.about.com
CIA Publications and Reports   www.odci.gov/cia/publications
The Library of Congress   www.loc.gov

yourDictionary.com www.yourdictionary.com
Refdesk www.refdesk.com

Poetry

Bartleby Verse: American & English Poetry 1250-1920 www.
bartleby.com/verse/
Internet Poetry Archive www.ibiblio.org/ipa/
Modern American Poetry www.english.uiuc.edu/maps/
Poetry Archives www.emule.com/poetry/
Poetry.com www.poetry.com
Poetry Daily www.poetrydaily.org
Poetry Magazine www.poetrymagazine.org/
Poets.org www.poets.org
Representative Poetry Online eir.library.utoronto.ca/rpo/display/
index.cfm

Public Domain Works

Aesop's Fables www.aesopfables.com/
African American Writers of the 19th Century digital.nypl.org/
schomburg/writers_aa19/
Alex Catalogue of Electronic Texts www.infomotions.com/alex/
The Avalon Project at Yale Univesity www.yale.edu/lawweb/avalon/
avalon.htm
Bartleby.com www.bartleby.com/
Bible Gateway (Bible in 40 languages) bible.gospelcom.net/versions/
Bibliomania: The Network Library www.bibliomania.com/index.html
The British Library www.bl.uk/onlinegallery/ttp/digitisation4.html
Digital Book Index www.digitalbookindex.com/
ClassicAuthors.net www.classicauthors.net/
The Complete Works of William Shakespeare www-tech.mit.edu/
Shakespeare/works.html
Duke Papyrus Archive scriptorium.lib.duke.edu/papyrus/
eScholarship Editions texts.cdlib.org/escholarship/
EServer.org eserver.org/
Folklore & Mythology Texts www.pitt.edu/~dash/folktexts.html
Institute for Learning Technologies www.ilt.columbia.edu/
publications/virgil.html
Internet Classics Archive classics.mit.edu/
The Latin Library www.thelatinlibrary.com/
Literature.org www.literature.org
The Online Books Page digital.library.upenn.edu/books/
The Online Classical and Medieval Library sunsite.berkeley.edu/
OMACL/
The Oxford Text Archive ota.ahds.ac.uk/
Perseus Project www.perseus.tufts.edu/cgi-bin/perscoll?type=text
Project Gutenberg promo.net/pg/index.html
Read Print www.readprint.com/
Smithsonian Institution Libraries www.sil.si.edu/DigitalCollections/
SunSITE Digitial Collections sunsite.berkeley.edu/Collections/
Univ. of California Press E-Books www.ucpress.edu/scan/
The Univ. of Chicago Press www.lib.uchicago.edu/eos/html/
Univ. of Michigan Humanities Text Initiative www.hti.umich.edu/
index-all.html
Univ. of Texas Libraries www.lib.utexas.edu/books/etext.html
Univ. of Virginia Library etext.lib.virginia.edu/collections/languages/

Publishers

Brookes Publishing   brookespublishing.com/
Dark Horse Comics   www.darkhorse.com
Harper Collins   www.harpercollins.com
Henry Holt   www.henryholt.com/
Houghton Mifflin   www.houghtonmifflinbooks.com/
Penguin Putman   www.penguinputnam.com
The Perseus Books Group   www.perseusbooksgroup.com/perseus/
home.jsp
Random House   www.randomhouse.com
St. Martin's Press   www.stmartins.com
Simon & Schuster   www.simonsays.com
Time Warner Bookmark   www.twbookmark.com/
Wiley   www.wiley.com
World Almanac   www.worldalmanac.com
W.W. Norton & Co.   www.wwnorton.com/trade/welcome.htm

Publishing Industry

American Book Association BookWeb.org   www.bookweb.org
Book Standard   www.bookstandard.com
Media Bistro   www.mediabistro.com
Publishing News (UK)   www.publishingnews.co.uk
Publishers Weekly   www.publishersweekly.com
Who Owns What?   www.cjr.org/tools/owners/

Quotations

AFI'S 100 Years...100 Movie Quotes   www.afi.com/tvevents/100years/
quotes.aspx
A Short Dictionary of Scientific Quotations   naturalscience.com/
dsqhome.html
Bartlett's Familiar Quotations   www.bartleby.com/

Short Stories

50 Word Fiction   fiftywordfiction.blogspot.com/

What's New on the Internet

Nerd World: Media (what's new in computer world) www.nerdworld.com/
whatsnew.html
Yahoo! What's New (listing of every new site each day; sometimes
thousands) : dir.yahoo.com/new

Writing Associations

Association of Writers & Writers Programs   www.awpwriter.org/
Author's Guild   www.authorsguild.org/
Horror Writers Association   www.horror.org/
Hurston/Wright Foundation   www.hurston-wright.org/
Mystery Writers of America   www.mysterywriters.org/
Publishing Triangle (Gay & Lesbian)   www.publishingtriangle.org
Romance Writers of America   www.rwanational.org/
Science Fiction & Fantasy Writers of America   www.sfwa.org/
Western Writers of America   www.westernwriters.org/
Writers Guild of America   www.wga.org/

Writing Tips

PoetryMagic   www.poetrymagic.co.uk/
Write4Kids.com   www.write4kids.com/index.html
Writers Weekly   www.writersweekly.com/
Writing.com   www.writing.com

READING GROUPS
Suggestions for Forming a Reading Group

1. **Size of Group:**
   How many people do you want for the group? Good group sizes range from 4 to12. But since meetings are generally held in the homes of the participants, the group size may well be dictated by the size of your living rooms. Members can include your friends, your family, and possibly others found by posting an ad.

2. **Purpose of Group:**
   Decide what the approach will be—will meetings involve in-depth analysis of the book, be mostly social gatherings with casual discussion, or be something in between?

3. **Number of Books:**
   How much of a reading load do you want? Most groups read one book for each meeting. The answer may affect your answer to the next question.

4. **Meetings:**
   How often do you want to meet, and where? While meetings are typically held in the homes of the participants (many groups take turns), a public site such as a coffee house, a community center, or a library may be a possibility. What time will you meet, and how long will you meet for? Scheduling a regular time and date helps people set aside the time. Will snacks be served, and if so, who will supply them?

5. **Book Choices:**
   You might want to start with a book you've read and enjoyed. Other suggestions can come from your local librarian, or from many available online sources (see below). Some groups rotate selections among members, while other groups make consensus decisions. Take into consideration that books available in paperback are more inexpensive and that some books may be more readily available in libraries. New books can be expensive if they are only available in hardcover.

6. **Contact List:**
   Create a contact list with the names, addresses, phone numbers, and e-mail addresses of the participants and decide on how members will be contacted.

7. **Leader:**
   Decide on whether you will have a single group moderator or will rotate this role among members.

8. **Discussion:**
   Many current books come with suggested questions for the specific book. Questions that might be discussed for many books include:
   a. What is the book about? Why did the author choose this subject?
   b. What was interesting about the plot or characters?
   c. What insights might you get from the book?
   d. Did you like the writer's style of writing?
   e. What do you know about the author?
   f. What kinds of reviews did the book get? Do you agree with what they say?
   g. Did you like the book? Why or why not?

9. **Enjoy!**

Reading Group Websites

Amazon.com Book Clubs: www.amazon.com/bookclub

Barnes & Noble: www.bn.com/bookclubs

Book Blog: www.bookblog.net

Book Browse: www.bookbrowse.com/reading_guides/

Book Clubs Resource.com: www.book-clubs-resource.com/

Book Spot: www.bookspot.com/readingguides.htm

Club Reading: www.clubreading.com/

Good Books Lately: goodbookslately.com/allaboutbookgroups.shtml

Great Books Foundation: www.greatbooks.org/typ/

Reading Group Choices: www.readinggroupchoices.com/

Reading Group Guide.com: www.readinggroupguides.com/

Target Bookmarked: bookmarked.target.com/

Yahoo Online Reading Group: groups.yahoo.com/group/
classicsreadinggroup/

Additionally, individual publishers often have websites associated with
the books they publish.

The 25 Best Lesbian and Gay Novels

Source: The Publishing Triangle (2005)

1. *Death in Venice*, Thomas Mann
2. *Giovanni's Room*, James Baldwin
3. *Our Lady of the Flowers*, Jean Genet
4. *Remembrance of Things Past*, Marcel Proust
5. *The Immoralist*, André Gide
6. *Orlando*, Virginia Woolf
7. *The Well of Loneliness*, Radclyffe Hall
8. *Kiss of the Spider Woman*, Manuel Puig
9. *The Memoirs of Hadrian*, Marguerite Yourcenar
10. *Zami*, Audre Lorde
11. *The Picture of Dorian Gray*, Oscar Wilde
12. *Nightwood*, Djuna Barnes
13. *Billy Budd*, Herman Melville
14. *A Boy's Own Story*, Edmund White
15. *Dancer from the Dance*, Andrew Holleran
16. *Maurice*, E.M. Forster
17. *The City and the Pillar*, Gore Vidal
18. *Rubyfruit Jungle*, Rita Mae Brown
19. *Brideshead Revisited*, Evelyn Waugh
20. *Confessions of a Mask*, Yukio Mishima
21. *The Member of the Wedding*, Carson McCullers
22. *City of Night*, John Rechy
23. *Myra Breckinridge*, Gore Vidal
24. *Patience and Sarah,* Isabel Miller
25. *The Autobiography of Alice B. Toklas*, Gertrude Stein

Oprah's Book Club Lists since 1996

1996

The Book of Ruth, Jane Hamilton

Song of Solomon, Toni Morrison

The Deep End of the Ocean, Jacquelyn Mitchard

1997

The Meanest Thing to Say, Bill Cosby

The Treasure Hunt, Bill Cosby

The Best Way to Play, Bill Cosby

Ellen Foster, Kaye Gibbons

A Virtuous Woman, Kaye Gibbons

A Lesson Before Dying, Ernest Gaines

Songs in Ordinary Time, Mary McGarry Morris

The Heart of a Woman, Maya Angelou

The Rapture of Canaan, Sheri Reynolds

Stones from the River, Ursula Hegi

She's Come Undone, Wally Lamb

1998

Where the Heart Is, Billie Letts

Midwives, Chris Bohjalian

What Looks Like Crazy on an Ordinary Day, Pearl Cleage

I Know This Much Is True, Wally Lamb

Breath, Eyes, Memory, Edwidge Danticat

Black and Blue, Anna Quindlen

Here on Earth, Alice Hoffman

Paradise, Toni Morrison

1999

A Map of the World, Jane Hamilton

Vinegar Hill, A. Manette Ansay

River, Cross My Heart, Breena Clarke

Tara Road, Maeve Binchy

Mother of Pearl, Melinda Haynes

White Oleander, Janet Fitch

The Pilot's Wife, Anita Shreve

The Reader, Bernhard Schlink

Jewel, Bret Lott

2000

House of Sand and Fog, Andre Dubus III

Drowning Ruth, Christina Schwarz

Open House, Elizabeth Berg

Poisonwood Bible, Barbara Kingsolver

While I Was Gone, Sue Miller

The Bluest Eye, Toni Morrison

Back Roads, Tawni O'Dell

Daughter of Fortune, Isabel Allende

Gap Creek, Robert Morgan

2001

A Fine Balance, Rohinton Mistry

The Corrections, Jonathan Franzen

Cane River, Lalita Tademy

Stolen Lives: Twenty Years in a Desert Jail, Malika Oufkir

Icy Sparks, Gwyn Hyman Rubio

We Were The Mulvaneys, Joyce Carol Oates

2002

Sula, Toni Morrison

Fall on Your Knees, Ann-Marie MacDonald

2003

East of Eden, John Steinbeck

Cry, The Beloved Country, Alan Paton

2004

One Hundred Years of Solitude, Gabriel García Márquez

The Heart Is a Lonely Hunter, Carson McCullers

Anna Karenina, Leo Tolstoy

2005

The Good Earth, Pearl S. Buck

As I Lay Dying, William Faulkner

The Sound and the Fury, William Faulkner

Light in August, William Faulkner

MISCELLANEOUS

Figures in the Hebrew Bible

Aaron: First of Hebrew high priests; brother of Moses and Miriam.

Abel: Second son of Adam and Eve; slain by Cain.

Abraham: Founder of Monotheism; patriarch; also called Abram (c. 13th cent. BCE)

Adam: First human according to Genesis.

Amos: Herdsman; prophesized against social injustice and oppression of the poor.

Bathsheba: Seduced by King David; mother of King Solomon.

Cain: Tiller of the soil; son of Adam and Eve; killed his brother Abel.

Cyrus: Persian Ruler; sent Jews home from exile (538 BCE).

Daniel: Cast into lion's den by Nebuchadnezzer; saved.

David: Israel's greatest king; shepherd, warrior, musician, psalmist (c. 1000 BCE)

Deborah: Prophet and Judge; ruled over Israel (c. 12-11th cent. BCE).

Elijah: Great Prophet; was victorious over the priests of the Phoenician god, Baal (9th cent. BCE).

Elisha: Prophet; successor to Elijah.

Esther: Jewish wife of the King of Persia; saved Jews from annihilation.

Eve: First woman according to Genesis.

Ezekiel: Visionary; prophesied hope to exiled Jews in Babylon.

Ezra: Great Jewish leader; (c. 516 BCE) rededicated worship and Torah law after exile.

Goliath: Giant Philistine warrior; slain by David.

Hannah: Childless; promised child to God; mother to the prophet Samuel.

Hosea: Enacted prophecy; asked God's forgiveness for Israel's unfaithfulness.

Isaac: Son of Abraham and Sarah; saved from sacrificial altar.

Isaiah: Highly educated prophet; avoided war with Assyria. Israel destroyed. Jerusalem survived.

Jacob: Son of Isaac; father of the Twelve Tribes; renamed "Israel" by angel.

Jeremiah: Confronted Leaders; urged surrender to Babylon.

Jezebel: Phoenician queen of King Ahab; had Israelite prophets killed.

Job: Blameless man; lost family and possessions but not his faith.

Jonah: Swallowed by a great fish; prophesied repentance in Nineveh.

Jonathan: Son of King Saul; friend of David.

Joseph: Favorite of Jacob; interprets Pharaoh's dreams; brings Hebrews to Egypt.

Josiah: Reformist king; repaired Temple; restored worship; reintroduced Passover. (640-609 BCE)

Joshua: Successor of Moses; led Hebrews into land of Israel.

Leah: Matriarch; older sister of Rachel; Jacob's wife and Joseph's mother.

Micah: Prophet; predicts the end of war and beginning of peace.

Miriam: Prophet and great leader of the Hebrews; sister to Moses and Aaron.

Moses: Most important Hebrew prophet; leader of the Israelites; received the Torah.

Nathan: Prophet; confronted King David over his seduction of Bathsheba.

Nebuchadnezzer: Babylonian King; destroyed Jerusalem (586 bce)

Nehemiah: Led Jews back to Jerusalem from Babylonian exile (432 bce)

Noah: A man of great faith who, according to *Genesis*, saved the world from the flood.

Rachel: Matriarch; younger sister of Leah; Jacob's wife; Joseph's mother.

Rebecca: Matriarch; wife of Isaac; mother of Jacob.

Ruth: Moabite convert; ancestor of David and all the kings of Israel.

Samuel: Prophet; anointed Saul king of Israel and later anointed David to succeed him.

Samson: Judge and military leader of Israel, possessing super-human strength (11th cent. bce).
Sarah: First Matriarch of Israel; wife of Abraham; mother of Isaac.
Saul: First king of Israel (1029-1005 BCE); father of Jonathan.
Solomon: King of Israel at its zenith; known for great wisdom.
Zachariah: Prophet; encouraged rebuilding of Temple destroyed by Babylonians.

Figures in the New Testament

Andrew: One of the Twelve Apostles; brother of Peter and former fisherman; one of the earlier disciples.
Barabbas: Imprisoned with Jesus; set free by Pilate on Passover.
Barnabas: Disciple of Jesus; closely connected with Paul.
Bartholomew: A lesser known member of the Twelve Apostles; cheerful and prayed often.
Cornelius: A Roman convert defended by Peter, allowing gentiles to become Christians.
Elizabeth: Mother of John the Baptist; relation of Virgin Mary.
Gabriel: Archangel; appears to the Virgin Mary as messenger from God.
Herod: Name used by kings at the time of Jesus. Two Herods appear in the New Testament: Herod the Great ordered the death of children around the time of Jesus's birth and his son, Herod, imprisoned John the Baptist leading to his beheading.
James: One of the Twelve; brother of John the apostle; close to Jesus.
Jesus: Central figure of the Gospels; believed to be the messiah and son of God; crucified by the Romans.
John (Baptist): Known as "John the Baptist"; important prophet and forerunner to Jesus; relation of Virgin Mary.
John (Apostle): One of the Twelve; possible author of Gospel of John; brother of James; considered pillar of the church.
Joseph: Husband of the Virgin Mary; descendant of King David; considered to be a just man.
Judas Iscariot: Betrayer of Jesus; former prominent member of the apostles; committed suicide.
Judas Thaddeus: One of the Twelve; also called "Jude" to distinguish him from Judas Iscariot.
Lazarus: Brother of the disciples Martha and Mary of Bethany; raised from the dead at their request; possibly the same Lazarus who appears in Jesus's parable of the rich man.
Luke: Traditional author of the Gospel of Luke; possibly a follower of Paul.
Mark: Traditional author of the Gospel of Mark; possibly the same Mark who is a companion of Peter.
Matthew: One of the Twelve; possible author of the Gospel of Matthew; a former tax collector.
Mary Magdalene: Important female disciple of Jesus; witness to his death and resurrection.
Mary, the Virgin: The mother of Jesus; believed to be a virgin without sin; wife of Joseph.
Matthias: Often included on lists of the Twelve Apostles as the apostle who replaced Judas Iscariot after his betrayal.
Paul (Saul): Writer of nearly a quarter of the New Testament; a former persecutor of Christians who is converted after a vision; played a significant role in spreading Christianity.
Peter: Considered to be the foremost of the Twelve Apostles; traditionally the first pope and "rock" of the Christian church; author of epistles; also called Simon and Simon Peter.
Philip: One of the Twelve; considered pragmatic and sensible.
Pilate, Pontius: A Roman prefect; plays large role in the trial and crucifixion of Jesus.

Simon: One of the Twelve; known as "the Zealot" to distinguish from Simon Peter.

Stephen: Fervently preaches that Jesus was the Messiah; stoned to death by angry mob, including Paul (Saul); important figure in Paul's conversion.

Thomas: One of the Twelve; known as "Doubting Thomas" because he did not believe Jesus was resurrected until he could touch him.

Timothy: A disciple closely connected with Paul; author of epistles.

Zechariah: Father of John the Baptist; husband of Elizabeth; struck dumb when his barren wife becomes pregnant.

Books of the Bible

Old Testament—Standard Protestant List*

Genesis	I Kings	Ecclesiastes	Obadiah
Exodus	II Kings	Song of Solomon	Jonah
Leviticus	I Chronicles	Isaiah	Micah
Numbers	II Chronicles	Jeremiah	Nahum
Deuteronomy	Ezra	Lamentations	Habakkuk
Joshua	Nehemiah	Ezekiel	Zephaniah
Judges	Esther	Daniel	Haggai
Ruth	Job	Hosea	Zechariah
I Samuel	Psalms	Joel	Malachi
II Samuel	Proverbs	Amos	

New Testament List

Matthew	II Corinthians	I Timothy	II Peter
Mark	Galatians	II Timothy	I John
Luke	Ephesians	Titus	II John
John	Phillippians	Philemon	III John
Acts	Colossians	Hebrews	Jude
Romans	I Thessalonians	James	Revelation
I Corinthians	II Thessalonians	I Peter	

* The standard Protestant Old Testament consists of the same 39 books as in the Bible of Judaism, but the latter is organized differently. The Old Testament used by Roman Catholics has 7 additional "deuterocanonical" books, plus some additional parts of books. The 7 are: **Tobit, Judith, Wisdom, Sirach (Ecclesiasticus), Baruch, I Maccabees,** and **II Maccabees**. Both Catholic and Protestant versions of the New Testament have 27 books, with the same names.

Top 25 Book-to-Film Box Office Hits

Source for box office figures: Internet Movie Database (www.imdb.com)

This table lists the top-grossing films of all time (in the U.S. as of March 5, 2005) that are based on books, along with the books that served as the source material.

Movie & Source	Box Office Gross* (in millions)
1. *The Lord of the Rings: The Return of the King* (2003) *The Return of the King* by J.R.R. Tolkien (1955)	$377.0
2. *The Passion of the Christ* (2004) The Bible	$370.3
3. *Jurassic Park* (1993) *Jurassic Park* by Michael Crichton (1990)	$356.8
4. *The Lord of the Rings: The Two Towers* (2002) *The Two Towers* by J.R.R. Tolkien (1955)	$340.5

5. *Forrest Gump* (1994) $329.7
   Forrest Gump by Winston Groom (1986)

6. *Harry Potter and the Sorcerer's Stone* (2001) $317.6
   Harry Potter and the Sorcerer's Stone by J.K. Rowling (1998)

7. *The Lord of the Rings: The Fellowship of the Ring* (2001) $313.8
   The Fellowship of the Ring by J.R.R. Tolkien (1954)

8. *Shrek* (2001) $267.7
   Shrek by William Steig (illustrator) (1990)

9. *Harry Potter and the Chamber of Secrets* (2002) $262.0
   Harry Potter and the Chamber of Secrets by J.K. Rowling (1999)

10. *How the Grinch Stole Christmas* (2000) $260.0
    How the Grinch Stole Christmas by Dr. Seuss (1957)

11. *Jaws* (1975) $260.0
    Jaws by Peter Benchley (1974)

12. *Harry Potter and the Prisoner of Azkaban* (2004) $249.3
    Harry Potter and the Prisoner of Azkaban by J.K. Rowling (1999)

13. *The Lost World: Jurassic Park* (1997) $229.1
    The Lost World by Michael Crichton (1996)

14. *The Exorcist* (1973) $204.6
    The Exorcist by William Peter Blatty (1971)

15. *Gone With the Wind* (1939) $198.7
    Gone With the Wind by Margaret Mitchell (1936)

16. *The Perfect Storm* (2000) $182.6
    The Perfect Storm by Sebastian Junger (1997)

17. *The Bourne Supremacy* (2004) $176.0
    The Bourne Supremacy by Robert Ludlum (1986)

18. *Tarzan of the Apes* (1999) $171.1
    Tarzan of the Apes by Edgar Rice Burroughs (1914)

19. *A Beautiful Mind* (2001) $170.7
    A Beautiful Mind by Sylvia Nasar (1998)

20. *Hannibal* (2001) $165.1
    Hannibal by Thomas Harris (1999)

21. *Catch Me If You Can* (2002) $164.4
    Catch Me If You Can by Frank W. Abagnale (1980)

22. *The Polar Express* (2004) $162.6
    The Polar Express by Chris Van Allsburg (1985)

23. *The Firm* (1993) $158.3
    The Firm by John Grisham (1991)

24. *True Lies* (1994) $146.3
    True Lies by Philip Ross (1988)

25. *I, Robot* (2004) $144.8
    I, Robot by Isaac Asimov (1950)

* All amounts are in USA dollars and only include theatrical box office re-
ceipts (movie ticket sales) and do not include video rentals, television
rights and other revenues. Totals may include theatrical re-release re-
ceipts. Figures are not adjusted for inflation.

Book Quiz: Clued into Books

Guess the real titles and authors from these clues. (Answers on page 96.)

1) The subsequent conflagration

Title: _____

Author: _____

2) Mona Lisa . . . - - - . . .

Title: _____

Author: _____

3) The closeted buzz

Title: _____

Author: _____

4) Get a tan and lose weight at the same time

Title: _____

Author: _____

5) Wee females

Title: _____

Author: _____

6) Self respect and narrow mindedness

Title: _____

Author: _____

7) Satisfying soil

Title: _____

Author: _____

8) The understood earth

Title: _____

Author: _____

9) Bright outlook

Title: _____

Author: _____

10) Mr. Welsh swivel hips

Title: _____

Author: _____

11) Commander of the Musca domestica

Title: _____

Author: _____

12) Husbandry place

Title: _____

Author: _____

13) The teeny royal

Title: _____

Author: _____

14) Feline in the fedora

Title: _____

Author: _____

15) Celsius 232.7777777777778

Title: _____

Author: _____

16) The era of naiveté

Title: _____

Author: _____

17) The inadvertent sightseer

Title: _____

Author: _____

18) Departed on a breeze

Title: _____

Author: _____

19) The splendid skeleton

Title: _____

Author: _____

20) Questioning an incubus

Title: _____

Author: _____

Cooking Books

Classic Cookbooks

Better Homes and Gardens New Cook Book, Better Homes and Gardens
The James Beard Cookbook, James Beard
Mastering the Art of French Cooking, Volume One, Julia Child, et al
The New York Times Cook Book, Craig Claiborne
Betty Crocker's Cookbook, Betty Crocker
The Fannie Farmer Cookbook, Marion Cunningham & Lauren Jarrett
Escoffier Cookbook, Auguste Escoffier
Larousse Gastronomique, Ed. Prosper Montague
The Gourmet Cookbook, Ed. Ruth Reichl
Joy of Cooking, Irma S. Rombauer and Marion Rombauer Becker

Celebrity Chefs & Cookbooks

La Cucina Di Lidia, Lidia Bastianich & Jay Jacobs
Simple Italian Food, Mario Batali
Cooking by Hand, Paul Bertolli
How to Cook Everything, Mark Bittman
Les Halles Cookbook, by Anthony Bourdain
I'm Just Here for the Food, Alton Brown
Michael Chiarello's Casual Cooking
Cat Cora's Kitchen
Cooking Thin with Chef Kathleen, Kathleen Daelemans
Paula Deen & Friends Living It Up, Southern Style
Everyday Italian, Giada De Laurentiis
Flavor, Rocco DiSpirito
Tom's Big Dinners, Tom Douglas
Bobby Flay's Grilling for Life
Eat This Book, Tyler Florence
Gale Gand's Just A Bite: 125 Luscious Little Desserts
The Barefoot Contessa Cookbook, Ina Garten
Madhur Jaffrey Indian Cooking
Today's Kitchen Cookbook, Ed. Laurie Dolphin
Bouchon, Thomas Keller
Complete Galloping Gourmet Cookbook, Graham Kerr
From Emeril's Kitchens, Emeril Lagasse
*How to be a Domestic Goddess: Baking and the Art of Comfort
     Cooking*, Nigella Lawson
Young & Hungry, Dave Lieberman
The Hassle-Free Host, Christopher Lowell
Cookies Unlimited, Nick Malgieri
The Balthazar Cookbook, Keith McNally, Riad Nasr & Lee Hanson
Sara Moulton Cooks at Home
The Naked Chef, Jamie Oliver
Cooking with the Two Fat Ladies, Jennifer Paterson & Clarissa
     Dickson Wright
Best of the Bake-Off Cookbook, Pillsbury
Jacques Pépin Fast Food My Way
Modern French Cooking for the American Kitchen, Wolfgang Puck
30-Minute Meals, Rachael Ray
The Zuni Café Cookbook, Judy Rodgers
Real Fast Food, Nigel Slater
George Stella's Livin' Low Carb
The Kitchen Sessions With Charlie Trotter
Blue Ginger: East Meets West Cooking with Ming Tsai
Martin Yan's Culinary Journey Through China

Travel

Traveling to one of the locations below? The recommended reading will give you a taste of the place.

Fiction

Afghantistan, 1975-2002, *The Kite Runner*, Khaled Hosseini

Alabama, 1930s, *To Kill a Mockingbird*, Harper Lee

Alaska, prehistory 18th century, *Alaska*, James Michener

Albany, NY, late 1930s, *Ironweed*, William Kennedy

Beijing, 1990s, *Lost in Translation*, Nicole Mones

Boston, MA, 17th century, *The Scarlet Letter*, Nathaniel Hawthorne

Burma, 1880s, *The Piano Tuner*, Daniel Mason

China, 1920, *The Good Earth*, Pearl S. Buck

Congo, 1950s, *The Poisonwood Bible*, Barbara Kingsolver

Cuba, 1940s, *Before Night Falls*, Reinaldo Arenas

Egypt, post-World War I, *Palace Walk*, Naguib Mahfouz

England, early 20th c., *Howards End*, E.M. Forster

Georgia and South Carolina, 1964, *Secret Life of Bees*, Sue Monk Kidd

Greece, the eve of World War II, *Colossus of Maroussi*, Henry Miller

Honduras, 1980s, *Mosquito Coast*, Paul Theroux

India, 1960s, *The God of Small Things*, Arundhati Roy

Israel, post-World War II, *Exodus*, Leon Uris

Japan, pre-World War II, *The Strangeness of Beauty*, Lydia Minatoya

Johannesburg, 1946, *Cry, the Beloved Country*, Alan Paton

Liberia and Georgia, 1910-40, *The Color Purple*, Alice Walker

Los Angeles, CA, 1950s, *LA Confidential*, James Ellroy

Long Island, NY, 1922, *The Great Gatsby*, F. Scott Fitzgerald

Mediterranean Sea, 1800, *Master and Commander*, Patrick O'Brian

Mexico, 1910, *Like Water for Chocolate*, Laura Esquivel

Newfoundland, 1990s, *The Shipping News*, E. Annie Proulx

New Mexico, mid-19th century, *Death Comes for the Archbishop*, Willa Cather

New York City, 1980s, *The Bonfire of the Vanities*, Tom Wolfe

New Zealand, 1976, *The Bone People*, Keri Hulme

Nigeria, 1890s, *Things Fall Apart*, Chinua Achebe

Nile River and Karnak, Egypt, 1930s, *Death on the Nile*, Agatha Christie

Normandy, France, 1850s, *Madame Bovary*, Gustave Flaubert

Oklahoma and California, 1930s, *The Grapes of Wrath*, John Steinbeck

Pittsburgh, PA, 1982, *The Mysteries of Pittsburgh*, Michael Chabon

Prague, Czechoslovakia, late 1960s, *The Unbearable Lightness of Being*, Milan Kundera

Sahara desert, late 1940s, *The Sheltering Sky*, Paul Bowles

Shanghai and San Francisco, CA, 1920s-90s, *The Kitchen God's Wife*, Amy Tan

Siberia, 1951, *One Day in the Life of Ivan Denisovich*, Alexander Solzhenitsyn

South America, 20th century, *The House of the Spirits*, Isabel Allende

St. Petersburg, Russia, 1860s, *Crime and Punishmen*, Fyoder Dostoyevesky

Tibet, 1930s, *Lost Horizon*, James Hilton

Nonfiction

Afghanistan, A *Short Walk in the Hindu Kush*, Eric Newby

Africa, *Out of Africa*, Isak Dinesen

Africa, *West With the Night*, Beryl Markham

Alaska, *Coming into the Country*, John McPhee

America, *Travels with Charley in Search of America*, John Steinbeck

Antarctica, *Terra Incognita: Travels in Antarctica*, Sara Wheeler

Asia, *The Great Railway Bazaar*, Paul Theroux

Australia, *In A Sunburned Country*, Bill Bryson

Balkans, *Through the Embers of Chaos*, Dervla Murphy

Calcutta, *Calcutta*, Geoffrey Moorhouse

Everest, *Into Thin Air: A Personal Account of the Mt. Everest Disaster*, Jon Krakauer

Florence, *Florence: A Delicate Case*, David Leavitt

France, *A Year in Provence*, Peter Mayle

Gabon, *One Dry Season*, Caroline Alexander

Himalayas, *The Snow Leopard*, Peter Matthiessen

Holy Land, *The Innocents Abroad*, Mark Twain

Istanbul, *Istanbul: Memories and the City*, Orhan Pamuk

Italy, *Under the Tuscan Sun: At Home in Italy*, Frances Mayes

Latin America, *The Motorcycle Diaries: Notes on a Latin American Journey*, Ernesto Che Guevera

Middle & Far East, *Travels with a Tangerine: From Morocco to Turkey in the Footsteps of Islam's Greatest Traveler*, Tim Mackintosh-Smith

Middle East, *Baghdad without a Map and Other Misadventures in Arabia*, Tony Horwitz

Patagonia, *In Patagonia*, Bruce Chatwin

Rio de Janiero, *Rio de Janiero*, Rua Castro

Sardinia: *Sea and Sardinia*, D.H. Lawrence

Siberia: *In Siberia*, Colin Thurbron

Southwest (U.S.) *Desert Solitaire: A Season in the Wilderness*, Edward Albee

Tibet, *Seven Years in Tibet*, Heinrich Harrer

Virginia, *Pilgrim at Tinker Creek*, Annie Dillard

World: *Travels: 1950-2000*, Jan Morris

World: *Around the World in 80 Days*, Michael Palin

World: *The Travels of Marco Polo*, Marco Polo

World: *Wind, Sand and Stars*, Antoine de Saint-Exupery

My Favorites

Favorite Authors

_____
_____
_____
_____
_____
_____
_____
_____

Favorite Lines

_____
_____
_____
_____
_____
_____
_____
_____

Books I Want to Read

_____
_____
_____
_____
_____
_____
_____
_____
_____
_____
_____

ANSWERS TO QUIZZES

Match the Book & Character on page 33

1. Atticus Finch—y. *To Kill A Mockingbird*, Harper Lee
2. Big Brother—a. *1984*, George Orwell
3. Captain Ahab—j. *Moby Dick*, Herman Melville
4. Celie—o. *The Color Purple*, Alice Walker
5. Dorothy Gale—x. *The Wizard of Oz*, L. Frank Baum
6. Ebenezer Scrooge—b. *A Christmas Carol*, Charles Dickens
7. Elizabeth Bennett—l. *Pride and Prejudice*, Jane Austen
8. Fagin—k. *Oliver Twist,* Charles Dickens
9. Hester Prynne—v. *The Scarlett Letter*, Nathaniel Hawthorne
10. Holden Caulfield—n. *The Catcher in the Rye*, J.D. Salinger
11. Holly Golightly—e. *Breakfast at Tiffany's*, Truman Capote
12. Howard Roark—p. *The Fountainhead*, Ayn Rand
13. Ichabod Crane—s. *The Legend of Sleepy Hollow*, Washington Irving
14. Ignatius J. Reilly—c. *A Confederacy of Dunces*, John Kennedy Toole
15. Jean Valjean—h. *Les Miserables*, Victor Hugo
16. Jo March—i. *Little Women*, Louisa May Alcott
17. Leopold Bloom—z. *Ulysses*, James Joyce
18. Lestat—g. *Interview with a Vampire*, Anne Rice
19. Madam DeFarge—d. *A Tale of Two Cities*, Charles Dickens
20. Natt Bumpo/Leatherstocking—. *The Last of the Mohicans*, James Fenimore Cooper
21. Nick and Nora Charles—w. *The Thin Man*, Dashiell Hammett
22. Philip Marlowe—m. *The Big Sleep*, Raymond Chandler
23. Sam Spade—t. *The Maltese Falcon*, Dashiell Hammett
24. Santiago—u. *The Old Man and the Sea*, Ernest Hemingway
25. Scarlett O'Hara—f. *Gone With the Wind*, Margaret Mitchell
26. Tom Joad—q. *The Grapes of Wrath*, John Steinbeck

Book Quiz on pages 90-91

1. The subsequent canflagaration: The Fire Next Time, James Baldwin
2. Mona Lisa . . . - - - . . .: The DaVinci Code, Dan Brown
3. The closeted buzz: The Secret Life of Bees, Sue Monk Kidd
4. Get a tan and lose weight at the same time: The South Beach Diet, Arthur Agatston
5. Wee females: Little Women, Louisa May Alcott
6. Self respect and narrow mindedness: Pride and Prejudice, Jane Austen
7. Satisfying soil: The Good Earth, Pearl S. Buck
8. The understood earth: The Known World, Edward P. Jones
9. Bright outlook: Great Expectations, Charles Dickens
10. Mr. Welsh swivel hips: Tom Jones, Henry Fielding
11. Commander of the Musca domestica: Lord of the Flies, William Golding
12. Husbandry place: Animal Farm, George Orwell
13. The teeny royal: The Little Prince, Antoine de Saint-Exupery
14. Feline in the fedora: The Cat in the Hat, Dr. Seuss
15. Celsius 232.7777777777778: Fahrenheit 451, Ray Bradbury
16. The era of naiveté: The Age of Innocence, Edith Wharton
17. The inadvertent sightseer: The Accidental Tourist, Anne Tyler
18. Departed on a breeze: Gone with the Wind, Margaret Mitchell
19. The splendid skeleton: The Lovely Bones, Alice Sebold
20. Questioning an incubus: Interview with a Vampire, Anne Rice